SURVIVAL
SECRETS

JOEY GREEN

128 INGENIOUS TIPS

TO ENDURE THE COMING APOCALYPSE
AND OTHER MINOR INCONVENIENCES

CHICAGO
REVIEW
PRESS

The author has conducted all the survival secrets in this book and has made every reasonable effort to ensure that they are safe when conducted as instructed. However, neither the author nor the publisher assumes any liability for damages caused or injury sustained from conducting these survival secrets.

A responsible adult should supervise any young reader who conducts the survival secrets in this book to avoid potential danger or injury.

Published by Chicago Review Press Incorporated
814 North Franklin Street
Chicago, Illinois 60610
ISBN 978-1-61374-985-2

Library of Congress Cataloging-in-Publication Data
Green, Joey.
  Last-minute survival secrets : 128 ingenious tips to endure the coming apocalypse and other minor inconveniences / Joey Green.
     pages cm
  Includes bibliographical references.
  ISBN 978-1-61374-985-2
  1. Survival—Miscellanea. 2. Handicraft—Miscellanea. 3. Emergency management—Miscellanea. 4. Consumer goods—Miscellanea. I. Title.

  GF86.G728 2014
  613.6'9—dc23
                              2014022852

Cover and interior design: Andrew Brozyna, AJB Design Inc.

Printed in the United States of America
5 4 3 2 1

For Laurie Abkemeier

CONTENTS

Introduction xi

1 GADGETS AND GIZMOS..1

How to Make a Life Vest from Condoms.. 2

How to Devise a Gas Mask with Vinegar and a Soda Bottle 5

How to Build a Solar-Powered Cooker with Aluminum Foil............... 8

How to Fashion an Impromptu Helmet with a Bucket 11

How to Make a Wi-Fi Antenna from a Coffee Can............................. 13

How to Boost a Cell Phone Signal with a Soda Can........................... 16

How to Produce a Fire Extinguisher with
Baking Soda and Vinegar 18

How to Assemble a Torch with
Tampons and Petroleum Jelly 20

How to Make a Trip Wire with Dental Floss 21

How to Detect a Trip Wire with Silly String 22

How to Make a Radio Antenna with a Slinky 23

How to Set Up a Burglar Alarm with Potato Chips........................... 25

How to Construct a Decoy with a
Bleach Jug and Bubble Wrap 26

How to Make a Smart Phone Stand with Binder Clips 28

How to Create a Postal Scale with a Ruler....................................... 30

How to Make a Rudimentary Copy Machine
with Vanilla Extract.. 31

How to Fashion a Battery from a Copper Scrubber........................... 32

How to Build a Flood Alarm with Aspirin and a Clothespin 33

How to Soundproof a Room with Egg Cartons.................................. 35

2 TRICKS OF THE TRADE..**37**

How to Start a Fire with Steel Wool and a Battery 38

How to Open a Locked Door with a Credit Card................................40

How to Pick a Lock with Bobby Pins 42

How to Start a Campfire with Potato Chips 45

How to Improvise Shoes with Rubber Gloves..............................47

How to Make Stilts with Plastic Paint Buckets 49

How to Create Boots with Duct Tape.....................................51

How to Write a Secret Message with Soap 53

How to Hide Valuables in a Tennis Ball,
Deodorant Stick, or Tampon 54

How to Make a Safe with a Hardcover Book........................57

How to Build a Wall Safe with an Electrical Socket 59

How to Cook Food with a Clothes Iron................................61

How to Brew Coffee Without a Coffee Maker.........................64

3 FOILED AGAIN **65**

How to Thwart a Terrorist with a Cell Phone 66

How to Slip Up an Attacker with Dishwashing Liquid 67

How to Create an Oil Slick with Vegetable Oil................................68

How to Blind an Evildoer with Cayenne Pepper.............................69

How to Disable a Car with Water 71

How to Improvise an Alarm System with a Mousetrap......................72

How to Rig Up an Alarm System with Bang Snaps 73

How to Open a Padlock with a Soda Can 74

How to Disable a Smoke Detector with Toothpaste..........................76

How to Break into a Locked Suitcase with a Ballpoint Pen 77

How to Tie Up a Bad Guy with Panty Hose..........................78

How to Make a Flame-Throwing Torch with Deodorant 80

4 SECRET WEAPONS 81

How to Make a Smoke Bomb with Sugar 82

How to Create a Stink Bomb with Ammonia 83

How to Create a Fireball with Flour 84

How to Create a Molotov Cocktail with Tampons 86

How to Fashion a Slingshot from a Bicycle Inner Tube 87

How to Build a Bola with Tennis Balls 88

How to Make a Knife from a Toothbrush 90

How to Make a Marble Gun with a Condom 92

How to Make a Smoke Screen with an Instant Cold Pack 93

How to Camouflage Yourself with Shoe Polish 95

How to Assemble an Emergency Kit with an Altoids Tin 96

How to Carve a Fake Gun from a Bar of Soap 98

How to Defend Yourself with a Ballpoint Pen 100

How to Make a Dart Gun from a Ballpoint Pen 101

How to Avoid Detection from Thermal Imaging
    Cameras with a Space Blanket 103

5 SURVIVAL TECHNIQUES 105

How to Protect Yourself from Nuclear Radiation with Iodine 106

How to Defend Yourself from a Biological Attack with a Bra 108

How to Prevent Heatstroke with a Disposable Diaper 109

How to Make Warm Clothes with a Bath Mat and Bubble Wrap 110

How to Make a Compass with a Cork and Needle 112

How to Make an Emergency Lantern with
    Baby Oil and a Tampon 114

How to Collect Rainwater with a Trash Bag 116

How to Desalinate Water with Plastic Wrap 118

How to Build a Water Purification Still with a Trash Bag 119

How to Make a Transpiration Still with a Trash Bag 121

How to Transport Water with a Cardboard Box 123

How to Filter Water with a Soda Bottle 124

How to Build a Stove with a Tuna Fish Can 126

How to Construct an Oven with Aluminum Foil
and Clothes Hangers 128

How to Build a Life Raft with Soda Bottles 130

How to Kindle a Fire with Chocolate and a Soda Can 132

How to Start a Fire with Petroleum Jelly and Cotton Balls 134

How to Pick Fruit from a Tree with a Bleach Jug 136

How to Catch Fish with Soda Bottles 138

How to Make a Fishing Rod with Dental Floss
and a Paper Clip 140

How to Devise a Fishing Net with Panty Hose 143

How to Build a One-Man Tent with Trash Bags 144

How to Assemble a Tube Tent with Trash Bags 146

How to Create an Emergency Toilet with Kitty Litter 148

How to Construct a Washing Machine with a Plunger 149

How to Make Soap with Ashes and Fat 151

How to Build a Solar-Powered Shower with a Trash Bag 153

How to Fashion a Signal Mirror from a Used CD 155

How to Put Together a Baby Mobile with Used CDs 157

How to Make Snow Goggles with a Cereal Box 158

How to Produce Snowshoes from Tennis Rackets 160

6 FIRST AID EMERGENCIES 161

How to Make a Signal Whistle with a Bottle Cap 162

How to Make a Signal Whistle with a Soda Can 163

How to Stop Bleeding from a Bullet Wound with Tampons 165

How to Recover from Diarrhea with Sugar,
Salt, and Lemon Juice 167

How to Disinfect a Knife Wound with Mouthwash............................ 169

How to Make Knee Pads with a Bra 171

How to Soothe Excruciating Toothache Pain with
Tabasco Sauce 173

How to Immobilize Broken Bones with a
Pizza Box and Bubble Wrap 175

How to Fashion a Sling from Panty Hose.. 177

How to Treat a Bee or Wasp Sting with a Credit Card
and Meat Tenderizer.. 178

How to Kill Head Lice with Mayonnaise... 180

How to Treat Poison Ivy with Nail Polish Remover 182

How to Remove Cactus Spines with Elmer's Glue 184

How to Soothe Severe Sunburn Pain with Iced Tea Mix 185

How to Treat Hypothermia with Aluminum Foil 187

How to Remove Broken Glass from Skin with Duct Tape 189

How to Stitch a Wound with Condoms and Dental Floss 191

7 DISASTER RELIEF 193

How to Make Flood Boots with Trash Bags 194

How to Build a Dike with Trash Bags 195

How to Boost a Cast-Iron Radiator with Aluminum Foil................... 197

How to Repair Broken Eyeglasses with Dental Floss 198

How to Make Homemade Laundry Soap with Borax 199

How to Find a Lost Contact Lens with Panty Hose 201

How to Get Rid of Mice and Rats with Fabric Softener 202

How to Repel Mosquitoes with Mouthwash 203

How to Make a Flyswatter with Duct Tape........................204

How to Warm Cold Sheets with a Soda Bottle..................206

How to Avoid Leeches with Panty Hose...........................207

How to Get Rid of Skunk Odor with Disposable Douche.................209

How to Seal Your Home from Chemical Weapons
    with Duct Tape 211

8 QUICK GETAWAYS 213

How to Start a Dead Car Battery with Aspirin 214

How to Revive a Dead Car Battery with Epsom Salt 215

How to Plug a Gas Tank Leak with Chewing Gum...........216

How to Repair a Broken Fan Belt with Panty Hose 217

How to Fix a Leaky Car Radiator with Black Pepper.......218

How to Clean Corrosion from Car Battery
    Terminals with Coca-Cola 219

How to Create Traction for a Car Stuck
    in Snow with Carpet Mats 221

How to Repair a Flat Tire with Superglue 222

Acknowledgments................................223
Bibliography 224
About Joey Green.............................228

Introduction

I magine the situation. You fall off a cruise ship in the middle of the ocean, or the ship unexpectedly smashes into an errant iceberg, gets hit by a tsunami and flips upside down, or capsizes after the drunken captain steers too close to shore and collides into underwater rocks. Unfortunately, you don't have a life vest. How do you make one while treading water?

While visiting Tahrir Square in Cairo, reoccupying Wall Street, or encountering the inevitable Martian invasion, you get a face full of tear gas, pepper spray, or heinous Martian vapor. Too bad you forgot your gas mask. What can you do besides cough and wheeze?

A massive hurricane knocks out the electricity for miles in every direction, making your electric stove and microwave oven useless. The torrential rain drenches all your firewood, and silly you forgot to fill the propane tank for the barbecue grill. How do you cook up some macaroni and cheese?

Fortunately, you can easily overcome any dire situation—during a natural disaster, terrorist attack, hostage crisis, or catastrophic emergency—by putting simple household items to use in unexpected ways. Yes, hundreds of quirky yet ingenious survival techniques are hidden in everyday household items.

In this book, you'll discover an abundance of handy and unusual secrets to outsmart the unexpected, escape perilous situations, and circumvent life-threatening dilemmas. You'll learn how to think like a resourceful, problem-solving survivalist, triumphing over complex emergency situations on the spot with everyday materials, instead of relying on months of preparation and expensive equipment. Should all hell break loose in the wake of a major disaster or calamity, you'll instinctively know how to make a radio antenna with a Slinky, revive a dead car battery with aspirin, and start a fire with potato chips.

Inside you'll discover how to defend yourself against intruders with dishwashing liquid, improvise an alarm system with dental floss, and make a flame-throwing torch with deodorant. You'll find step-by-step instructions on how to use everyday products to construct the tools needed to escape harrowing situations and survive unforeseen cataclysms—using ingenuity to transform common objects into rescue devices. You'll learn how to make a life vest with condoms, build a solar-powered cooker with aluminum foil, start a fire with steel wool and a battery, hide valuables in a tennis ball, fashion a sling with panty hose, and build an emergency lantern with baby oil and a tampon.

How did I discover all these offbeat survival secrets? Growing up in Florida, I lived through several hurricanes, stood in the eye of the storm, and experienced days without electricity. While backpacking around the world on our honeymoon, my wife and I fled the military occupation of La Paz, Bolivia. Shortly after we moved to Los Angeles, the 1994 Northridge earthquake ravaged our apartment. While visiting New York City on September 11, 2001, we witnessed the terrorist attack on the World Trade Towers and wound up stranded in the city for a week. To survive, I've broken into my own locked suitcase with a ballpoint pen, filtered and purified puddle water with a bandana and iodine, treated dehydration with a disposable diaper, cooked food with a clothes iron, carried an emergency kit inside an Altoids tin, disinfected a wound with Listerine mouthwash, and splinted a broken leg with a pizza box and Bubble Wrap. You can too. All you need is the gumption to live by your wits. And perhaps a paper clip and a pair of panty hose.

By the way, if you ever find yourself in the midst of a third-world revolution or postapocalyptic hellhole, return to your hotel room, fill the bathtub with water, and then go to the hotel bar and buy all the bottles of liquor. The filled bathtub becomes your emergency water supply, and you can use the alcohol as an anesthetic, an antiseptic, fuel to start a fire, or—should the economy completely collapse—the new currency. Cheers!

1

GADGETS AND GIZMOS

You can't get cell phone reception. Your burglar alarm goes on the fritz. You desperately need a helmet. Fortunately, a slew of seemingly innocuous household items—an empty soda can, a bag of potato chips, or a simple mop bucket—can be used to create an extensive arsenal of handy gadgets.

How to Make a Life Vest from Condoms

WHAT YOU NEED

- Two condoms
- Two shoelaces (or 3-foot length of dental floss)

WHAT TO DO

1. Unwrap the first condom, unroll it, place your lips against the opening, and inflate as if it were a balloon. When the condom reaches roughly 18 inches in diameter, tie a double knot in the free end.
2. Tie one end of a shoelace above the knot of the inflated condom and knot it securely several times.
3. Repeat with the second condom, fastening one end of the second shoelace to just above the knot.
4. Tie the free ends of the shoelaces together securely.
5. Holding one inflated condom in your left hand, guide the second condom under your left arm, around your back, and under your right arm. Position the inflated condoms at the height of your chest.
6. Enter the water slowly to prevent the inflated condoms from popping, or the dental floss from breaking. (If you can enter the water only by jumping, do not assemble the life vest until you are in the water.)

HOW IT WORKS

Once you are in the water with the life vest around your body, the water displacement created by the inflated condoms will keep you afloat. The condoms, made from sturdy latex, are surprisingly rugged and will not pop.

ALWAYS WEAR A LIFE VEST WHEN BOATING

The US Coast Guard estimates that life jackets could have saved the lives of more than 80 percent of the people killed in boating accidents. Most boating accidents happen with terrifying speed on the water, giving individuals little time to reach for a stowed life jacket. Life jackets designed to keep your head above water can prevent you from drowning should you be knocked unconscious and overboard during a boating accident. A snug-fitting life vest can also help you survive in cold water, insulating your body and preventing hypothermia.

STAYING AFLOAT

- To make an effective lifesaver (a buoyant device, not the candy), fill a clean, empty bleach jug with an inch of water, secure the cap in place, and tie a rope to the handle. Holding the free end of the rope, toss the jug to the drowning person. The water gives the jug just enough weight so you can toss the jug a significant distance.
- Improvise a more substantial lifesaver by knotting a piece of rope around the handles of four clean, empty bleach jugs. Secure the caps in place and tie the ends of the rope together to form a loop, which can then fit around a person's waist.
- In a dire emergency, you can improvise a float from an ice chest or cooler (sealed shut, with duct tape, if necessary), a plastic trash bag filled with air and knotted (or twist tied) shut, or even a bucket (or large plastic salad bowl) turned upside down and submerged to trap air inside.

EVERY TRICK IN THE BOOK
The Condom Conundrum

A condom can save your life—in more ways than one.

- **Cell Phone Case.** Insert your cell phone into a condom to create a waterproof case.
- **Fishing Bobber.** Inflate a condom slightly, tie a knot in the open end, and tie it to your fishing line as a bobber.
- **Fuse Protectors.** During the Vietnam War, SEALS used condoms as sheaths to keep fuse igniters dry and ready.
- **Ice Pack.** Fill a condom with water, like a water balloon, tie a knot in the open end, and place in the freezer to create an emergency ice pack.
- **Match Container.** A condom doubles as a waterproof container for matches.
- **Rifle Sheath.** To keep debris or rainwater out of the barrel of a rifle, place a condom over the muzzle.
- **Sterile Glove.** Wear a condom on your hand or around several fingers to treat a wound and prevent infection.
- **Tinder Box.** Store dry fire tinder inside a condom to protect it from wet or rainy weather conditions.
- **Water Container.** Fill a condom with water, like a water balloon, to transport or store water in this expandable container.

How to Devise a Gas Mask with Vinegar and a Soda Bottle

WHAT YOU NEED

- Scissors
- 1-liter plastic soda bottle
- Handful of cotton balls
- 1 cup of vinegar (apple cider vinegar is less pungent than white vinegar, but both work equally well)

WHAT TO DO

1. Using a pair of scissors, cut the soda bottle diagonally across the bottom so that the bottle, when placed against your face, fits snugly over your nose and mouth.
2. Holding the uncapped bottle upside down, fill the bottle halfway with cotton balls.
3. Saturate the cotton balls with vinegar.
4. Place the bottom of the bottle over your mouth and nose (making sure you have a tight seal against the skin), and breathe through the bottle.
5. For eye protection, wear shatterproof swim goggles (also available with prescription lenses) that provide an excellent seal. To prevent the goggles from fogging up and inhibiting your vision, coat the inside of the lenses with a drop of shaving cream and then buff clean.
6. Never wear contact lenses if you anticipate being exposed to tear gas or pepper spray.
7. Wear long pants, a long-sleeved shirt, and a hat to prevent chemicals from coming in contact with your skin.

Bonus Tip: If you want to keep your hands free, use duct tape (folded in half lengthwise) to fashion a strap to hold the soda bottle in place over your nose and mouth.

HOW IT WORKS

Vinegar neutralizes and counteracts the effects of tear gas and pepper spray. As early as 77 BC, Roman naturalist Pliny the Elder noted the beneficial effects of vinegar on respiratory problems.

SIMPLE GAS MASK

For a more impromptu version, simply soak a bandana in vinegar and keep it in a ziplock storage bag until you need it. To use, hold the vinegar-soaked bandana over your nose and mouth and breathe through it. You can wear a disposable respirator mask underneath the bandana to avoid breathing the vinegar directly.

YOUR CUP RUNNETH OVER

If you desperately need a simple dust mask, take a bra and place a single cup over your nose and mouth, holding it in place to create a tight seal against your face. The various materials blended and tightly knit together to make bras—cotton, foam, Jacquard, latex, mesh, microfiber, nylon, polyester, satin, spandex, Spanette, and tricot—are similar to those used in disposable dust masks sold in hardware stores.

CHEMICAL WEAPONS

The two most common chemical weapons used by police are tear gas (chloroacetophenone) and pepper spray (capsicum oleoresin). Mace is usually an aerosol form of tear gas or a mixture of tear gas and pepper spray. The best way to protect your eyes and lungs from tear gas is to wear a gas mask with shatterproof lenses, such as US M17 masks.

- **Tear Gas.** Tear gas—a chemical irritant—sticks to skin, combines with body oils to create an acidic solution that causes minor burns on the skin, and causes a burning sensation in the eyes, nose, mouth, and lungs. It can cause serious respiratory distress. Tear gas is typically dispersed from a canister to create a fog or mist.

- **Pepper Spray.** Pepper spray—a concentrated extract from hot peppers—causes an extremely painful burning sensation in the eyes, throat, nose, and skin. If inhaled or ingested, pepper spray can cause respiratory disorder. It is generally sprayed from a small aerosol can or a fogger resembling a fire extinguisher.

IF YOU'RE EXPOSED TO TEAR GAS

1. If you are exposed to tear gas or pepper spray, leave the area immediately, find fresh air, and breathe. You should feel better right away.

2. If your breathing remains strained, assume that your lungs have been contaminated, consider this a respiratory emergency, and seek immediate medical attention or call 911. Sit upright until help arrives, taking slow breaths.

3. If you are exposed to tear gas, Mace, or pepper spray in the eyes, remove contact lenses immediately to avoid permanent eye damage. Flush the eyes with water and seek medical attention immediately.

4. Remove contaminated clothes as soon as possible, place them in a plastic bag, seal it closed, and discard it.

5. Shower in cold water (to keep your pores closed) and scrub vigorously with castile soap. Wash your hair with castile soap without allowing chemicals in your hair to get on your face.

6. If you experience any discomfort in your eyes or with your breathing, seek medical attention.

How to Build a Solar-Powered Cooker with Aluminum Foil

WHAT YOU NEED
- Ruler
- Pencil
- Large sheet of corrugated cardboard (3 feet by 4 feet)
- Utility knife
- Spoon
- White school glue
- Water
- Paintbrush (at least 1 inch wide)
- Aluminum foil
- 2 clothespins

WHAT TO DO

1. Using the ruler and pencil, measure and draw the shape shown in the diagram on the sheet of corrugated cardboard.

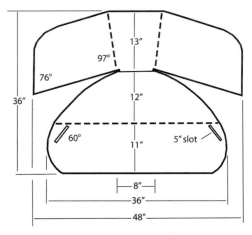

2. Use a utility knife to carefully cut the sheet of cardboard as shown in the diagram. Make the slots slightly narrower than the thickness of the cardboard so that the flaps will fit snugly.

3. Score the fold lines with a blunt edge of the spoon handle (using the ruler as a guide, if necessary).

4. Fold the cardboard against the ruler (or a firm, straight edge, like the edge of a tabletop) according to the diagram.

5. Mix equal parts white glue and water. Paint the diluted glue onto the dull side of sheets of aluminum foil, enough to cover the entire

inside surface of the cardboard panel. Smooth the foil onto the panel. Leave flat to dry.

6. To set up the oven as shown, lay the panel flat with shiny side up. Fold up front and back parts and insert the two end flaps back into the slots in front.

7. Clamp a clothespin onto the underside of each flap, near the slot, to hold them in place.

HOW TO COOK FOOD

1. Place your food in a black cooking pot with a tight-fitting lid. You can use this simple solar-powered oven to cook food, bake breads, and pasteurize water.

2. Place the pot inside a clear, heat-resistant plastic bag (such as an oven bag), and close the open end of the bag. If you don't have an appropriate bag, cover the pot with a clear glass bowl.

3. Place the bag-enclosed pot in the center of the flat part of the solar oven panel.

4. Place the solar-powered cooker in direct sunlight for several hours. For a noontime meal, start cooking the food by 9:00 or 10:00 AM. For an evening meal, start cooking the food by 1:00 or 2:00 PM.

5. Use potholders to remove the pot (which will be very hot) from the plastic bag.

HOW IT WORKS

When exposed to sunlight, a dark-colored cooking pot converts light energy to heat energy, which starts cooking the food inside the pot. The aluminum foil panels reflect additional sunlight onto the pot, increasing the temperature. The clear plastic bag acts as a heat trap, allowing additional sunlight in while retaining the heat.

Cooking food using this solar-powered oven generally takes about twice as long as using a conventional oven. The temperature inside the pot gradually increases, allowing you to leave the food unwatched as it slowly cooks. Once the food is cooked, the oven simply keeps it warm—without burning it. This means you never have to stir the food while it cooks. The oven usually reaches a maximum temperature of 300°F as the food nears completion.

The solar-powered cooker will cook food as long as the temperature inside the pot reaches approximately 200°F. The high temperatures recommended in cookbooks for conventional ovens simply cook foods faster.

RECIPES

- **Baking.** Depending on the amount of dough, allow 1 to 1.5 hours for breads and biscuits. Allow 1 hour for cookies.
- **Beans.** Soak the beans in water overnight, and then cook with water for 2 to 3 hours.
- **Beef, Chicken, or Fish.** Place in the pot without any water. For beef, allow between 1.5 and 3 hours (depending on the size). For chicken, allow between 1.5 and 2.5 hours. For fish, allow 1 to 1.5 hours.
- **Cereals and Grains.** Add two parts water for every one part rice, wheat, barley, or oats. Let soak for 2 or 3 hours before cooking. Cook for 1 hour, shake the pot to guarantee uniform cooking, and then cook for another 30 minutes to 1 hour.
- **Pasta and Dehydrated Soups.** Heat the water for roughly 1 hour to achieve a temperature near boiling. Add the pasta or soup mix, stir well, and then cook for another 15 to 20 minutes.
- **Vegetables.** Cut fresh carrots, broccoli, potatoes, etc. into equal-sized pieces to promote uniform cooking. Place in the pot without any water. Allow 1.5 hours to cook.

MAKING WATER SAFE TO DRINK

Contrary to popular belief, water does not have to be boiled to be safe to drink. Heating water to 150°F for 20 minutes pasteurizes the water, making it safe to drink. Pasteurization kills all human disease pathogens, without wasting the energy needed to bring the water to a boil. If you don't have a thermometer to ensure that the water has reached 150°F, boiling the water guarantees that the water temperature is at least 212°F.

How to Fashion an Impromptu Helmet with a Bucket

WHAT YOU NEED
- Clean, empty plastic bucket
- Pencil
- Scissors
- Sheet or acetate from clear plastic folder
- Duct tape
- Foam or bubble wrap (optional)

WHAT TO DO

1. Place the bucket on your head, and then, using the pencil, draw a line from the rim of the bucket to the height of your eyebrows to make rectangular shapes to be cut from the bucket, leaving a nose guard.

2. Using the scissors, cut out the rectangles, removing any excess plastic to customize the size of the helmet.

3. Cut the sheet of acetate from a clear plastic folder, making sure it is large enough to fit inside the bucket and cover the rectangular cutouts. Using duct tape, attach the acetate to the inside of the plastic helmet.

4. For greater protection and comfort, pad the inside of the jug with foam rubber, Styrofoam, or Bubble Wrap.

5. Use the bucket handle as a loose chin strap, or to make a more secure chin strap (to prevent the helmet from flying off your head during an accident), tear off a 6-inch length of duct tape, fold it in half lengthwise (sticking the tape to itself), and then use additional strips of duct tape to adhere each end of the chin strap to the inside sides of the bucket.

HOW IT WORKS

Wear the bucket jammed tightly over your head and ears. The plastic provides protection from the talons of birds and the claws of animals, and the helmet doubles as a rudimentary hard hat, though far less sturdy than the real thing.

USING YOUR HEAD

- To prevent head and brain injuries, wear an appropriate helmet whenever you ride a bicycle, ski, or participate in activities that make your head vulnerable to injury (such as in-line skating, sledding, baseball, and rock climbing).
- A helmet made from a plastic bucket does not meet the standards of the Consumer Product Safety Commission or the Snell Memorial Foundation.
- Motor vehicle accidents killed 677 bicyclists in the United States in 2011 and injured an additional 48,000 others that same year, according to the National Highway Traffic Safety Administration. Wearing a bicycle helmet reduces the risk of serious head and brain injury by 25 to 55 percent, according to a study published in 2011 in *Accident Analysis and Prevention*.
- During a blow to the head, a helmet—a hard shell padded on the inside with thick, rigid foam, such as polystyrene—absorbs a great deal of the force of impact, cushioning the blow.
- In 2010 in the United States, roughly 400 bicycle riders under the age of 20 were killed and an estimated 207,500 sustained bicycle-related injuries that required emergency care. Annually, 26,000 of these bicycle-related injuries to children and adolescents are traumatic brain injuries treated in emergency departments, according to the Centers for Disease Control and Prevention.
- Never wear a helmet when climbing a tree or playing on playground equipment. A helmet may get stuck on a tree limb or a piece of playground equipment and cause strangulation.

How to Make a Wi-Fi Antenna from a Coffee Can

WHAT YOU NEED

- Clean, empty Dole Pineapple Juice or Campbell's Tomato Juice can (46 fluid ounces)
- Soldering iron
- Solder
- Ruler
- Indelible marker
- Drill with ⅝-inch and ⅛-inch bits
- N-type female connector (UHF SO-239 Chassis-Mount Coaxial Connector Socket—available at Radio Shack)
- 2-inch length of 12-gauge copper wire
- Wire cutters
- 4 sets of #6-32 x ½-inch screws and nuts
- Pigtail (a Wi-Fi antenna cable with a male reverse polarity SMA connector with a female inner sleeve contact—to connect the N-type female connector to the external antenna connector on a wireless card)
- Wireless card with an external antenna connector (with an output of at least 200 milliwatts)

- Metallic 4-inch to 6-inch air-conditioning duct adapter—available at the Home Depot or Lowe's (optional)
- Duct tape or aluminum foil tape (optional)

WHAT TO DO

1. Remove the top of the can and the paper label.

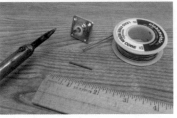

2. Solder a piece of copper into the N connector.

3. On the side of the can, measure $1^{11}/_{16}$ inches (43 mm) from the bottom of the can and make a mark with an indelible marker.

4. Using the ⅝-inch bit, drill a hole in the side of the can large enough to mount the N connector in place. (To prevent the can from being crushed when you drill, fill the can halfway with water, place the can in your freezer, and when the water freezes to ice, remove the can and drill the holes. The ice helps the can retain its shape. Let the ice melt and dry the can before continuing further.)

5. Using the base of the N connector as a template and the ⅝-inch bit, drill four holes in the side of the can to accommodate the screws to mount the N connector in place.

6. Cut a piece of straight copper wire and solder it to the N connector so that the height of the wire is $1^{7}/_{32}$ inches (31 mm) after you insert the N connector into the hole in the side of the can.

7. Mount the prepared N connector to the can with the screws and nuts.

8. Connect the appropriate end of the pigtail to the N connector.

9. Connect the other end of the pigtail wire to the antenna port on your wireless card.

10. Turn on your computer's Wi-Fi and point the can in whatever direction best increases the level of Wi-Fi reception on your computer. Rotate the can slowly to find the angle with the strongest signal.

11. To double the signal strength of the "cantenna" (adding 3 decibels), attach a metallic 4-inch to 6-inch air-conditioning duct adapter to the open end of the can. Slide the 4-inch-wide end of the adapter over the can to create a trumpetlike bell, and secure in place with duct tape or aluminum foil tape.

HOW IT WORKS

A 46-ounce can of Dole Pineapple Juice or Campbell's Tomato Juice is a standard no. 3 cylinder can with a diameter of 4.25 inches and a height of 7 inches—the perfect size for a homemade directional antenna to receive a 15-decibel bandwidth at 2.4 gigahertz without experiencing severe signal loss. The homemade cantenna significantly boosts your computer's Wi-Fi reception in whatever direction the opening of the can faces, capturing Wi-Fi signals broadcast from farther distances.

DOWN TO THE WIRE

- Technically, using a homemade cantenna is illegal. Federal Communications Commission (FCC) regulations—Part 15.247—permit Americans to use only FCC-approved antennas.
- When you're not using the antenna, store the cable and adapter inside the can.
- Pringles cans are too narrow to receive Wi-Fi radio wavelengths, and the can is actually made from cardboard, not metal. The faux metallic coating on the inside of the canister does not conduct electricity or receive Wi-Fi radio waves.

How to Boost a Cell Phone Signal with a Soda Can

WHAT YOU NEED

- Ruler
- Indelible marker
- Clean, empty soda can
- Work gloves
- Tin snips (or sharp scissors)
- Pliers
- Piece of foam rubber, Styrofoam, or Bubble Wrap (3 inches in diameter)
- Headset or Bluetooth earpiece (optional)

WHAT TO DO

1. Using the ruler and indelible marker, draw a straight, vertical line from the top of the can down the length of the can to the bottom of the can.

2. Holding your cell phone up to the can, mark the height of your cell phone on the vertical line you previously drew on the can.

3. Starting and finishing at the mark indicating the height of your cell phone, draw a line around the can (perpendicular to the length of the can).

4. One-half inch from the bottom of the can, draw another line around the can (again, perpendicular to the length of the can).

5. Using the tin snips and wearing work gloves (to avoid cutting yourself on the metal), cut off the top of the can to the height of the cell phone.

6. Cut along the line from the top of the can to the line at the bottom of the can.

7. Cut along the line circling the bottom of the can, except for 1 inch on the side of the can directly opposite the original vertical line. The sides of the can will spread open like wings, forming a crescent.

8. Using the pliers, crimp the sharp edges of the can (including the cutout bottom of the can) by folding over the edge and compressing it, creating a hem to avoid cutting yourself on the can.

9. Place a piece of foam rubber, Styrofoam, or Bubble Wrap inside the bottom of the can to create a cushion base for the cell phone.

10. Attach a headset or Bluetooth earpiece to your cell phone (or put it on speaker phone), stand the cell phone inside the can, and position the open wings of the can toward the nearest cell phone tower.

11. Turn on the phone and make a call.

HOW IT WORKS

The soda can doubles as a parabolic reflector, boosting the ability of the cell phone's internal antenna to receive cellular signals.

HOLD THE PHONE

Here are a few other ways to boost the reception on your cell phone antenna:

- **Aluminum Foil (or Aluminum Foil Tape).** Remove the battery cover from the back of the cell phone, fold up a piece of aluminum foil, place it on top of the battery, and replace the cover. The aluminum foil will increase reception by one or two bars. Or instead of using a folded piece of aluminum foil, adhere a strip of aluminum foil tape (available at hardware stores) on the inside of the battery cover. Turn on the phone. The signal strength should increase by a few bars.

- **Coffee Can.** Use a pigtail cord (compatible with your cell phone) to attach a coffee can Wi-Fi antenna (see page 13) to the antenna connector on your cell phone (typically located under a rubber casing on the back of your mobile phone).

- **Paper Clip.** Find the external antenna jack on the backside of your cell phone, typically covered by a small rubber casing. Pry off the rubber cover to reveal a coaxial connector jack. Take a metal paper clip and straighten the outer loop. With a pair of needle-nose pliers, bend ¼ inch of the end of the paper clip at a 90-degree angle. Insert the bent end of the paper clip into the coaxial connector on your cell phone and let the paper clip rest on the backside of your phone. Secure the paper clip in place with a small piece of masking tape or duct tape (or even a small adhesive bandage).

- **Twist Tie.** If you have a small exterior antenna on your cell phone, wrap a twist tie (containing a metal wire) around the antenna completely and secure it in place with electrical tape (or a small adhesive bandage). The twist tie boosts your reception approximately fourfold.

How to Produce a Fire Extinguisher with Baking Soda and Vinegar

WHAT YOU NEED
- 1 cup of vinegar
- Clean, empty glass jar with lid
- Paper towels
- Rubber band
- 2 tablespoons of baking soda

WHAT TO DO
1. Pour the vinegar into the jar.
2. Use a sheet of paper towel to carefully wipe any splashed vinegar from inside of the top half of the jar.
3. Place a clean sheet of paper towel over the mouth of the jar and push the center of the towel into the jar to a small pocket or cup approximately 1 inch deep.
4. Wrap a rubber band around the mouth of the jar to hold the paper towel in place.
5. Place 2 tablespoons of baking soda into the cup formed by the paper towel inside the mouth of the jar.
6. Screw the lid on the jar, without letting the vinegar wet the paper towel inside the jar.
7. In case of fire, shake the jar vigorously, aim the mouth of the jar at the base of the flames, and open the lid.

HOW IT WORKS
The combination of baking soda and vinegar produces carbon dioxide, a gas heavier than air. The carbon dioxide covers the flame and prevents the fire from getting any oxygen, which extinguishes the fire.

WHERE'S THE FIRE?
- Red fire extinguishers contain pressurized carbon dioxide, which, when sprayed at a fire, deprives the fire of its oxygen supply, putting out the flames.

- Carbon dioxide puts out electrical fires, fires caused by combustible liquids and gases, and fires caused by common combustibles like wood, paper, and clothes.
- Pouring baking soda over a grease fire extinguishes the flames. The sodium bicarbonate—the ingredient in baking soda and Class K fire extinguishers—does the trick.
- Every year, the Colonial Theatre in Phoenixville, Pennsylvania, hosts Blobfest, a celebration of the 1958 cult science fiction movie *The Blob*. The festivities include the annual Fire Extinguisher Parade—to honor the firefighting equipment from the local high school that actor Steve McQueen and the town's teenagers used in the movie to freeze the gelatinous amoeba-like alien and save the world from the Blob.

WHERE THERE'S SMOKE, THERE'S A FIRE EXTINGUISHER

In 2008, when his girlfriend ignored his request not to smoke, a 42-year-old antismoker in Bielefeld, Germany, emptied an entire fire extinguisher to put out the cigarette, coating the woman and their shared apartment in white powder. "My colleagues said it looked like a bomb had gone off in there," a spokesman for the Bielefeld police told Reuters. "He managed to put the cigarette out though."

How to Assemble a Torch with Tampons and Petroleum Jelly

WHAT YOU NEED
- Tampon
- Wire coat hanger
- Wire
- Petroleum jelly
- Butane lighter or matches

WHAT TO DO
1. Open the wrapper, take out the tampon, and remove the cardboard or plastic applicator, placing it aside for later use.
2. Hold the hook atop the wire coat hanger with one hand, and with the other hand pull down the middle of the base of the wire triangle, to straighten the triangle into a long, looped handle.
3. Slide the end of the wire handle into the cardboard or plastic applicator tube (to serve as an insulated sheath for the handle).
4. Straighten the hook.
5. Skewer the tampon on the end of the straightened hook, like a marshmallow at the end of a stick.
6. Wrap wire around the tampon to hold it to the coat hanger.
7. Coat the tampon with petroleum jelly.
8. Holding the wire handle by the cardboard (or plastic) handle, use the butane lighter or matches to ignite the tampon.

HOW IT WORKS
The cotton tampon, saturated with petroleum jelly, burns for a long time.

SOAK IT UP
For tinder to start a fire, pull apart a tampon or maxi pad to create a bundle of fluff, and use matches or a butane lighter to ignite it.

How to Make a Trip Wire with Dental Floss

WHAT YOU NEED
- Dental floss

WHAT TO DO
1. Tie one end of a long piece of dental floss around the leg of a bed 4 inches above the floor.
2. Tie the other end of the dental floss to a dresser leg across the room— 4 inches above the floor—and make sure the dental floss is taut.
3. Turn out the lights in the room.

HOW IT WORKS
When an intruder or assailant walks swiftly across the room, the dental floss will cause the perpetrator to trip and fall to the floor.

HAVE A SAFE TRIP
- To use a grenade as a booby trap, soldiers tie one end of a trip wire to a zero-second delay grenade, remove the safety pin, and place the grenade in an empty tin can (which holds the strike lever in place). When the enemy crosses the trip wire, the wire pulls the grenade from the can, and the grenade explodes. Other times, soldiers tie the trip wire to the pull ring on the grenade and then secure the grenade to an object. When the enemy trips the wire, the wire pulls out the safety pin, and the grenade explodes.
- In the 1963 movie *The Great Escape*, Hilts (Steve McQueen) strings a trip wire across a rural road, wrapping it around two road posts on the sides of the road. The trip wire knocks a German soldier off his motor-cycle, which Hilts steals to speed away toward Switzerland.
- On August 31, 2013, Daniel Ricketts, a 50-year-old marijuana grower in Berne, New York, accidentally rode a quad bike into a neck-high trip wire made of piano wire strung to protect his plants, throwing him off the ATV and nearly cutting off his head. The county coroner pronounced Ricketts dead at the scene.
- On September 19, 2013, a nighttime jogger accidentally ran into a trip wire maliciously tied at chest height across a footbridge in Exeter, England. The jogger flew backward, hit her head, and suffered a serious neck injury. The police are determined to bring the perpetrator to justice.

How to Detect a Trip Wire with Silly String

WHAT YOU NEED

- 1 or more cans of Silly String

WHAT TO DO

1. If you suspect that an area might be booby-trapped with trip wires, spray the area from side to side with Silly String.
2. If the Silly String falls to the ground, there are no trip wires in that area. If the Silly String appears suspended in the air on invisible wires, the Silly String marks the trip wire.

HOW IT WORKS

Silly String, a long, colored streamer of foam that shoots up to 12 feet from an aerosol can, drapes over invisible trip wires without setting them off due to the light weight of the foam string.

NO STRINGS ATTACHED

- In October 2008, Army Specialist Todd Shriver, stationed in Iraq, telephoned his mother in Stratford, New Jersey, and explained that US Marines had taught his unit how to use Silly String on patrol to detect booby traps. Unfortunately, the military did not provide Silly String to soldiers as standard equipment. After sending some cans to her son, Marcelle Shriver enlisted the help of her church, raising donations of money and cans  of Silly String. Upon learning that US postal regulations prohibited Shriver from shipping the potentially hazardous aerosol cans by air through the postal service, a private pilot agreed to fly the 1,000 cans to Kuwait, where they would then be taken to Iraq.

- In 1972, Robert P. Cox and Leonard A. Fish developed a foamable resin that could be sprayed from an aerosol can to create a cast over a broken arm or leg. When testing nozzles for the can, Fish discovered one nozzle that shot a long string of plastic foam across the room. He realized that a less sticky version of the string in various colors would make an excellent toy. Cox and Fish licensed their invention to Wham-O, the toy company that marketed the Hula Hoop and Frisbee.

How to Make a Radio Antenna with a Slinky

WHAT YOU NEED

- Double-sided alligator clip (or wire)
- Slinky (metal)
- Length of string, twine, or clothesline rope, 20 feet long
- 2 lengths of string, twine, or clothesline rope, 2 feet each

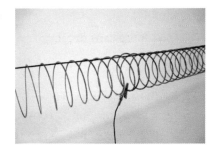

WHAT TO DO

1. To make a radio or television antenna with a Slinky, attach one end of a double-sided alligator clip to one end of the spring toy and attach the other end of the double-sided alligator clip to the existing radio or television antenna.

2. Tie one end of the 20-foot length of string, twine, or clothesline rope to a door hinge, tree branch, or other projection near the radio or television set.

3. Thread the free end of the 20-foot length of string through the compressed Slinky, stretch the string taut across the room or outdoor area, and then tie the free end to another door hinge, tree branch, ceiling rafter, or other projection, creating a horizontal line.

4. Tie one end of a 2-foot length of string around the last two coils on end of the Slinky attached to the alligator clip and tie the other end of the string around the nearby door hinge, tree, ceiling rafter, or other projection.

5. Tie one end of the second 2-foot length of string around the last two coils on the free end of the Slinky, stretch the Slinky 15 feet across the length of the horizontal line, and tie the free end of that string around the second door hinge, tree, ceiling rafter, or other projection.

HOW IT WORKS

The horizontal string keeps the stretched helical coils of the Slinky horizontal and unencumbered by any interference. A classic metal Slinky stretched anywhere between 5 feet and 15 feet has inductance, and resonates as a quarter wave between 7 and 8 megahertz. The helical coil slows wave velocity, altering phase shift along the length of the antenna and improving directivity.

SPRING INTO ACTION

- The Slinky antenna is compact, portable, and easy to set up and dismantle.
- To get the dipoles in the Slinky to resonate at frequencies above 7 and 8 megahertz, use an alligator clip, binder clip, or clothespin to clip a few of the spirals in the coil together.
- To obtain multiband frequencies, stretch two Slinky coils end to end across the area and attach the adjoining ends of the two Slinky coils together with a coaxial wire or twin lead. Then attach one end of a double-sided alligator clip to the coaxial wire and attach the other end of the double-sided alligator clip to the existing radio or television antenna.
- During the Vietnam War, communications soldiers would toss a Slinky over a high tree branch as a makeshift radio antenna.
- A Slinky can be stretched 25 feet without being bent out of shape.
- In 1985, Space Shuttle astronaut Jeffrey Hoffman became the first person to play with a Slinky in zero-gravity physics experiments while in orbit around the Earth.
- In a department store, walk onto an up escalator, set a Slinky on the step behind you, and halfway up the escalator, flip the top coil of the Slinky to the next lower step so the Slinky starts walking down the stairs of the escalator. If the escalator moves at the same speed as the Slinky, the Slinky will continue walking down the escalator forever.
- Standing on a ladder, hold a Slinky by one end and let the other end hang down without touching the ground. When you drop the Slinky, will the bottom end spring upward? Or will the bottom end fall to the ground first? Or will the bottom end stay where it is until the entire Slinky has compressed, and then fall to the ground?

How to Set Up a Burglar Alarm with Potato Chips

WHAT YOU NEED
- Bag of potato chips

WHAT TO DO

1. Open the bag of potato chips and pour them on the floor under a window or inside a door, making sure the potato chips are spread out over a 2-foot-square area.
2. Stay clear of the area.

HOW IT WORKS
When an intruder enters through a window or door, he or she will step on the potato chips, making a loud crunching sound, alerting you to his or her presence.

WHEN THE CHIPS ARE DOWN
- If you don't have any potato chips, you can also make this burglar alarm with Fritos corn chips, pretzels, Doritos, tortilla chips, raw macaroni noodles, or any solid food that makes a loud crunch when stepped on.
- At four o'clock in the morning on January 11, 2009, a man walked into a 76 gas station in Tracy, California, grabbed two bags of potato chips, brandished a revolver, and demanded cash from the register. When the cashier ran to the backroom, the robber left with the chips and drove away without any cash from the register.
- On July 5, 2012, police arrested 21-year-old Benjamin Sickles for breaking into a Subway sandwich shop in Washington County, Pennsylvania, at 2 AM and stealing nine bags of potato chips. Police followed a trail of potato chip bags from the store to the suspect sitting on the steps of Washington High School.
- Snack companies have created odd potato chip flavors, such as Walkers Cajun Squirrel Potato Crisps (Great Britain), Walkers Lamb & Mint Potato Crisps (Great Britain), Calbee Seaweed and Salt Potato Chips (Japan), Herr's Heinz Ketchup Flavored Potato Chips (United States), and Walkers Chilli & Chocolate Potato Crisps (Great Britain).
- In the 2013 movie *Reds 2*, a character pours a can of Pringles potato crisps inside a door as an impromptu burglar alarm.

How to Construct a Decoy with a Bleach Jug and Bubble Wrap

WHAT YOU NEED

- Clean, empty bleach jug
- Broomstick
- Duct tape
- Pair of panty hose
- Baseball cap
- Clothes hanger
- Long-sleeve shirt
- Bubble Wrap or newspaper
- Pair of long pants
- Safety pins, clothespins, or binder clips
- Pair of latex dishwashing gloves
- Pair of shoes
- Pair of socks (optional)

WHAT TO DO

1. Place the bleach jug upside down on the end of the broomstick and secure in place with a strip of duct tape.
2. Pull the waist of a clean, used pair of panty hose over the base of the jug and braid the legs to create a wig of hair.
3. Put the baseball cap over the base of the jug.
4. Attach the clothes hanger to the broomstick just under the mouth of the bleach jug to create shoulders for the decoy.
5. Fit the long-sleeve shirt on the hanger, button it up, and fill with crumpled-up sheets of Bubble Wrap or newspaper to make the torso and arms.
6. Stuff the pants with crumpled up sheets of Bubble Wrap or newspaper to make the abdomen and legs, tuck the shirt into the pants, and attach them together with safety pins, clothespins, or binder clips.
7. Stuff crumpled sheets of Bubble Wrap or newspaper inside a pair of latex dishwashing gloves and attach the gloves to the ends of the shirtsleeves with safety pins, clothespins, or binder clips.

8. Place a pair of shoes or boots at the bottom of each pant leg, or fill a pair of socks with crumpled Bubble Wrap or newspaper, attach them to the bottom of each pant leg with safety pins, clothespins, or binder clips, and then place the shoes on the socks.

HOW IT WORKS

The presence of a human decoy can lure an adversary into danger or, conversely, frighten away a potential intruder. A human decoy can also divert an attacker's attention, giving you the ability to counterattack from another position or flee the situation unnoticed.

DUMMY UP

- For centuries, humans have used scarecrows to scare away crows that would otherwise feed on newly planted seeds and growing crops.
- Hundreds of towns and villages around the world host annual scarecrow festivals, featuring scarecrows erected in gardens, in open spaces, in hidden corners, and on rooftops.
- In May 1940 during World War II, German airborne forces used straw-filled paratrooper dummies (known as paradummies) to make the German invasion of Belgium look larger and more threatening. The German Airborne also used straw-filled dummies as fake paratroopers during the Battle of the Bulge.
- The British dropped dummy paratroopers over North Africa and Italy in 1940, over Madagascar in 1942 (against the Vichy French to divert attention away from amphibious assaults elsewhere), and similarly along the French coast during the D-Day invasion on June 6, 1944.
- The best-known scarecrow in the world is arguably the Scarecrow in L. Frank Baum's novel *The Wonderful Wizard of Oz* and the 1939 movie *The Wizard of Oz*. The Scarecrow, stuffed with straw, accompanies Dorothy on her journey down the Yellow Brick Road in the hopes that the Wizard will bestow him with a brain.
- The Scarecrow, a comic book supervillain created in 1941 by Batman creators Bill Finger and Bob Kane, appeared in the movies *Batman Begins* (2005), *The Dark Knight* (2008), and *The Dark Knight Rises* (2012).
- In 2008, the 1,700 residents of Hoschton, Georgia, built 5,441 scarecrows to triple the town's population and break the Guinness World Record for "Most Scarecrows in One Location." Before that, the Cincinnati Horticultural Society set the record at the 2003 Cincinnati Flower and Farm Fest, with 3,311 scarecrows.

How to Make a Smart Phone Stand with Binder Clips

WHAT YOU NEED

- 3 medium-sized binder clips
- Business card

WHAT TO DO

1. Clip one binder clip along the long edge of the business card near one corner.
2. Clip a second binder clip along that same long edge of the business card near the opposite corner.
3. Extend the arms of the two binder clips flat against both sides of the business card.
4. Clip the third binder clip in the center of the opposite long edge of the business card, between the extended arms.
5. Leave the two arms of the third binder clip in their upright position.
6. Place the assembly flat on a desktop or counter.

7. Set the smart phone horizontally with its back against the centered binder clip arm that creates a back stand and the bottom edge of the phone against the stop created by the two binder clips.

HOW IT WORKS

The slot created between the binder clips provides a space to contain the smart phone, and the upright arm created by one of the binder clips furnishes a backrest for the device.

TAKE A STAND

- To make the smart phone stand more elaborate, attach two binder clips like horizontal wings to the one upright binder clip serving as the backrest.
- To make a smart phone stand from a paper clip, straighten out a large paper clip and bend it into the shape shown at right.

- You can also make a smart phone stand with a plastic cassette tape holder. Simply open the cassette tape holder completely, set the box on the tabletop surface, and rest the smart phone in the slot designed to hold the cassette tape.

- To make a smart phone stand from toy building bricks such as Legos, you'll need one 6-peg-by-8-peg flat plate, two 1-peg-by-8-peg bricks, and five 2-peg-by-8-peg bricks. (Smaller bricks combined into the same dimensions, as in the photo, will also work.) Snap the two 1-by-8 bricks together and snap the stack along one side of the plate. Snap the five 2-by-8 bricks on top of each other and snap the stack to the other side of the plate. Stand the smart phone upright in the slot created by the two stacks of Lego building bricks, leaning against the tall stack.

How to Create a Postal Scale with a Ruler

WHAT YOU NEED

- Pencil
- 12-inch ruler
- 5 quarters

WHAT TO DO

1. Place the pencil on a flat surface.
2. Lay the ruler across the pencil at the 6-inch mark, forming a cross and turning the ruler into a miniature seesaw.
3. Place the letter you wish to weigh on one side of the ruler, with the center of the letter over the 9-inch mark.
4. Place a stack of five quarters on the 3-inch mark on the ruler.

HOW IT WORKS

A stack of five quarters weighs 1 ounce. If the side of the ruler with the quarters on it touches the table, the letter weighs less than 1 ounce and requires one first-class stamp. If the side of the ruler with the envelope on it touches the table, the letter weighs more than 1 ounce and requires more than one first-class stamp. You can add five more quarters to the stack to determine whether the letter requires more than two first-class stamps.

SMALL CHANGE

If you don't have five quarters, the following combinations of coins also weigh roughly 1 ounce:

- 3 quarters, 5 dimes (1.00 ounce)
- 2 quarters, 1 dime, 3 nickels (1.00 ounce)
- 2 quarters, 1 dime, 2 nickels, 2 pennies (1.00 ounce)
- 1 quarter, 10 dimes (1.00 ounce)
- 1 quarter, 4 nickels, 1 penny (0.99 ounce)
- 11 pennies (0.97 ounce)
- 8 pennies, 2 nickels (0.99 ounce)

How to Make a Rudimentary Copy Machine with Vanilla Extract

WHAT YOU NEED

- 1 teaspoon of vanilla extract
- 1 teaspoon of dishwashing liquid
- Bowl
- Spoon
- Sponge, paintbrush, or cotton swab
- Document to be copied
- Clean sheet of paper (the same size or larger than the document)

WHAT TO DO

1. Mix the vanilla extract and dishwashing liquid together in a small bowl with the spoon.
2. With a sponge, paintbrush, cotton swab, or your fingers, cover the ink on the document you wish to copy with a thin coat of the solution.
3. Place the clean sheet of paper over the original document and press down firmly.
4. Using the spoon, burnish the back of the clean sheet of paper.
5. Carefully peel the two sheets of paper apart to reveal a mirror image of the original document.

HOW IT WORKS

The mixture of vanilla extract and dishwashing liquid, applied to the original document, acts as a solvent, liquefying the dry ink. When the two sheets of paper are pressed together, some of the ink from the original penetrates the second sheet, creating a reverse image. To read the copy, simply turn it over, hold the printed side up to the light, and read it through the back. You can also read its reflection in a mirror.

DO YOU COPY?

If the ink on the original document is suitably dark, you should be able to print several copies using this method.

How to Fashion a Battery from a Copper Scrubber

WHAT YOU NEED
- Wire cutters
- 2 feet of electrical wire
- Copper scouring pad
- Paper towels
- White vinegar
- Aluminum foil

WHAT TO DO
1. Use the wire cutters to cut the electrical wire in half and strip 1 inch from both ends of the two pieces of wire.
2. Secure one end of one of the wires to the copper scouring pad.
3. Saturate a sheet of paper towel with vinegar and then wrap it tightly around the copper pad.
4. Wrap a sheet of aluminum foil tightly around the paper towel.
5. Attach one end of the second wire to the aluminum foil.

HOW IT WORKS
The vinegar (containing acetic acid) is the electrolyte, the cooper scouring pad is the anode, and the aluminum foil is the cathode, creating a wet cell battery with modest voltage.

RECHARGE YOUR BATTERIES
- In the 1790s, Italian scientist Count Alessandro Volta made the first battery by stacking pairs of silver and zinc disks separated from one another by cardboard disks moistened with a salt solution. The volt, a unit of electric measurement, is named after him.

- To boost the copper scouring pad battery, fill a clean, empty jar with vinegar and submerge the aluminum-foil-wrapped scouring pad in the jar. You can also wire several of these cells together in series to increase the voltage.

How to Build a Flood Alarm with Aspirin and a Clothespin

WHAT YOU NEED

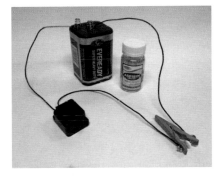

- Wooden spring-activated clothespin
- Drill with ⅛-inch bit
- 2 sets of #6-32 x ½-inch screws and nuts
- Wire cutters
- 3 feet of electrical wire
- 6-volt battery
- 6-volt DC buzzer (70 decibels)
- Aspirin tablet
- Duct tape or contact glue

WHAT TO DO

1. Disconnect the clothespin spring from the two wooden prongs.
2. At the spot on one of the slats where the two prongs snap shut, drill a small hole through the ump. Insert a screw (so the head will face inside the clothespin) and gently secure it in place with the nut.
3. Repeat step 2 with the second wood prong so that the heads of the two screws make contact when you put the clothespin back together.
4. Reassemble the clothespin.

5. Use the wire cutters to cut the electrical wire into three 1-foot sections, and strip 1 inch from both ends of the three pieces of wire.
6. Loosen one of the nuts on the clothespin and wrap one end of one of the wires to the threads of the screw under the nut, tightening the nut to secure it in place.
7. Repeat step 6 with a second wire and second screw on the clothespin.
8. Attach the free end of one of the wires from the clothespin to one of the terminals on the 6-volt battery.
9. Attach one end of the third wire from the remaining terminal on the 6-volt battery and attach the free end of that same wire to the buzzer.

10. Attach the free end of the remaining wire attached to the clothespin to the buzzer. With the two screw heads making contact between the clothespin prongs, the buzzer will sound.

11. Squeeze the clothespin open, position an aspirin tablet between the two screw heads, and gently allow the wooden prongs to close, holding the aspirin tablet in place between the two screw heads. The aspirin tablet prevents the two screw heads from making contact.

12. Set the clothespin on the floor of a basement (securing one of the wooden legs to the floor with a strip of duct tape or contact glue), and place the battery and buzzer bell on slightly higher ground.

HOW IT WORKS

The heads of the two metal screws touch each other, completing the circuit and sounding the buzzer. Placing an aspirin tablet between the two heads of the screws breaks the circuit. If the basement should start to fill with water, the water will dissolve the aspirin tablet, causing the spring-activated clothespin to snap the metal screw heads together, completing the circuit again and allowing electricity from the battery to trigger the buzzer.

HOLD IT TOGETHER

- David M. Smith invented the spring-activated, two-piece clothespin in 1853 in Springfield, Vermont. In the patent application for his two-piece clothespin, Smith explained that his newfangled clothespin, unlike the one-piece clothespin, could not "be detached from the clothes by the wind as is the case with the common pin and which is a serious evil to washerwomen."

- In 1887, another Vermont inventor, Solon E. Moore, improved upon Smith's design with the "coiled fulcrum," a single wire forming the spring hinge that joins the two slats of wood together.

- In 1974, American pop artist Claes Oldenburg sculpted a 45-foot-tall steel sculpture of a clothespin, which stands at Centre Square in Philadelphia and suggests two lovers hugging and kissing.

How to Soundproof a Room with Egg Cartons

WHAT YOU NEED

- Dozens of clean, empty cardboard egg cartons (collected from family and friends)
- Scissors
- Staple gun

WHAT TO DO

1. Move the furniture to the center of the room and remove all framed artwork from the walls.
2. Open an empty egg carton and, using a pair of scissors, carefully cut off the lid and the flap.
3. Start at the edge of one wall at the upper or lower corner and use the staple gun to firmly attach the egg carton bottom to the wall with the bottom of the egg carton facing out, so you see the bumpy backsides of the egg compartment dimples.
4. Cut the lid and flap off a second cartoon. Place the egg carton bottom next to the first carton, overlapping the edges, and staple it to the wall.
5. Continue cutting the lid and flap off the cartons and stapling them to the wall in straight rows and columns until you have covered the wall with egg cartons.
6. Repeat the process on each wall and on the ceiling.

HOW IT WORKS

Attaching egg cartons to the walls of a room does not actually soundproof the room. The cardboard (or foam) does not absorb sound effectively. However, egg cartons do reduce *echo* just as effectively as expensive acoustic foam. Normally, sound bounces off a wall, heads toward the opposite wall, and then bounces back continually, until the sound waves dissipate. The cardboard absorbs some of the sound, and the shape of the egg cartons disperses the reflected sound waves, scattering them about the room, minimizing any echo. While egg cartons on the walls certainly look low budget, they also give the room a flatter frequency response and a lower overall level of reverberation.

SOUND OFF

- State-of-the-art acoustic paneling usually adorns the walls of concert halls and recording studios to minimize sound waves bouncing off flat surfaces.
- Many garage bands insist that adhering egg cartons to the walls does provide a form of soundproofing that outperforms bare walls.
- Sheets of soundproofing foam shaped like egg cartons and purchased to insulate walls is both more effective and costlier than using the cardboard egg cartons. Unlike egg cartons, soundproofing foam is also fire resistant.
- To collect egg cartons with ease, ask a restaurant for its leftover industrial-sized cardboard egg trays, which typically hold 30 eggs.
- Newspaper editor Joseph L. Coyle of Smithers, British Columbia, invented the egg carton in 1911 to end a dispute. A local farmer was shipping eggs to a hotel in Aldermere, British Columbia, and the eggs frequently arrived broken. To stop the farmer and hotel owner from blaming each other, Coyle designed an egg carton made from paper to protect the eggs during their journey from the farm to the hotel.

2

TRICKS OF THE TRADE

Can you start a fire without matches or a butane lighter? Do you know how to open a locked door without a key? In a pinch, where can you inconspicuously hide your valuables? How do you heat up a can of soup without a stove or microwave oven? Get ready to learn some shrewd techniques.

How to Start a Fire with Steel Wool and a Battery

WHAT YOU NEED

- Steel wool pad
- 9-volt battery
- Tinder
- Kindling

WHAT TO DO

1. Pull the steel wool pad apart until it is all fuzzy and the size of a tennis ball.
2. Place the steel wool fuzz ball where you intend to build your fire.
3. Touch the ends of the battery to the steel wool.
4. When the steel wool catches fire and starts to glow red hot, add tinder and kindling and gently blow at the steel wool to start a flame.

HOW IT WORKS

Electrical resistance causes the steel wool to spark and glow red hot, and the iron filings from the steel wool sparkle like a Fourth of July sparkler. The iron threads in the steel wool, surrounded by oxygen, easily combust.

PLAYING WITH FIRE

- The steel wool never actually ignites into a flame. Instead, the iron threads turn into glowing embers, which can be used to blow tinder into a flame.
- Steel wool requires roughly 3 volts of electricity to spark and turn into embers. A single AA or AAA battery supplies only 1.5 volts of electricity and will not ignite steel wool. However, two AA or AAA batteries placed in series (end to end, with the positive end of one battery touching the negative end of the other battery) provide the necessary 3 volts and will ignite steel wool.
- Most cell phone batteries deliver more than 3 volts and will ignite steel wool. Some new cell phone batteries, however, contain a protection circuit that prevents the battery from being short-circuited, which touching the terminals to steel wool does.

- When carrying a 9-volt battery, you can prevent keys, coins, or a pen in your pocket from crossing the battery terminals by carrying the battery inside a sealed, empty plastic prescription pill bottle.
- If you don't have any steel wool, you can kindle a fire with a battery and a short piece of insulated electrical wire. Use a pair of wire cutters to cut the electrical wire in half, and strip 1 inch from both ends of the two pieces of wire. Connect the end of one wire to the positive post on the battery; connect the end of the second wire to the negative post. Twist the two remaining ends of wire together. The two ends twisted together will start to heat up and glow orange. Touch the glowing ember to tinder and blow gently to ignite a fire. Once the fire starts up, **take the battery away from it.**
- If you're stranded in the middle of nowhere with a car, you can start a campfire with jumper cables and the car battery. Place some tinder on the ground, carefully attach the jumper cables to the battery terminals, and strike the positive and negative leads together over the tinder. The resulting spark should ignite the tinder. To make the tinder more flammable, before connecting the jumper cables to the battery, mix ¼ teaspoon of gasoline (***no more!***) with the tinder and let it sit for a minute to allow the gas fumes to rise. When you strike the leads of the jumper cable together over the prepared tinder, the gas fumes should ignite instantly.

ADDING FUEL TO THE FIRE

To siphon gasoline from a motor vehicle, place an empty container on the ground, uncap the gas tank, and insert a clear tube (1 inch in diameter and long enough to reach from the bottom of the gas tank to the can on the ground) into the gas tank. Gently suck on the free end of the tube (without inhaling any gas fumes or getting any gasoline in your mouth), and when you see the fuel in the clear tube nearing your mouth, stop sucking and crimp the end of the tube. Place the end of the tube into the container on the ground, let go of your crimp, and gas will flow into the container. When you have enough gas in the container, pull the tube from the gas tank and let the gas in the tube empty into the container.

How to Open a Locked Door with a Credit Card

WHAT YOU NEED
- Credit card or plastic gift card
- Scissors

WHAT TO DO
1. Make sure the lock you wish to open is a spring bolt lock. You can use a credit card to open a spring bolt lock, not a dead bolt lock.
2. Choose a credit card or other laminated card that you don't mind damaging.
3. Wedge the card into the gap between the door and the jamb beside the doorknob latch. (If molding prevents you from sliding the card into the space, use a crowbar to pry off the molding.)
4. Simultaneously wiggle and push the credit card toward the latch in the gap between the door and the jamb. If the angled side of the latch faces away from you, utilize the method outlined below.
5. While pushing the card inward, bend the card away from the doorknob. When you feel the credit card push the spring bolt back into the door, turn the doorknob.

FOR A LATCH WITH THE ANGLE FACING AWAY
1. If the angled side of the latch faces away from you, use a pair of scissors to cut the credit card into the shape of the letter L, with each leg being 1 inch wide.
2. With the bottom left-hand corner of the L facing upward, wedge the bottom leg of the L into the gap between the door and the jamb just above the doorknob latch.
3. Holding the top end of the long leg of the L, wiggle and push the credit card down so that the short leg of the L goes in behind the latch.
4. Slowly pull the credit card toward you, bending the card away from the doorknob. When you feel the short leg of the L push the spring bolt back into the door, turn the doorknob.

HOW IT WORKS
The credit card forces the lock to release.

BEHIND CLOSED DOORS
- Breaking into and entering another person's apartment, dorm room, or house is illegal, unless you have express permission to do so.
- A spatula, knife, or flat-head screwdriver can be used like a credit card to pry aside the tongue of a locked door.
- In the mystery novel *Burglars Can't Be Choosers* by Lawrence Block, burglar Bernie Rhodenbarr opens the door to his motel room without a key, "utterly ruining a credit card in the process."

How to Pick a Lock with Bobby Pins

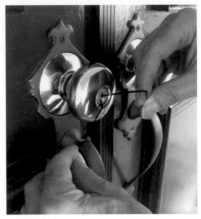

WHAT YOU NEED

- 2 bobby pins
- Butane lighter or matches

WHAT TO DO

1. Open the legs of one bobby pin to make them straight and then bend ½ inch at the end of the straight leg (as opposed to the wiggly leg) of the bobby pin to form a 90-degree angle. Use a butane lighter or matches to melt off the plastic tip on the bent end of bobby pin. The bent bobby pin is your tension wrench.

2. Open the second bobby pin to form a 90-degree angle. Use a butane lighter or matches to melt off the plastic tip on the end of the straight leg. The straight leg is your pick.

3. Insert the short end of the tension wrench into the bottom of the keyhole. Using the tension wrench, try to twist the cylinder slightly clockwise and then slightly counterclockwise, paying attention to the firmness of the stop in each direction. Whichever direction the stop has the most give is the direction the cylinder turns to be unlocked with a key.

4. Twist the tension wrench slightly in the direction that the cylinder opens. The cylinder should turn only a fraction of an inch. Hold the tension wrench in place, applying slight pressure. This keeps the pins protruding inside the cylinder and lined up with their housings.

5. Insert the pick into the top part of the keyhole and use the end of the pick to feel the five to seven pins protruding down from the ceiling of the cylinder. Pushing up slightly on any one of the pins raises it back up into its housing. Releasing the pin allows the spring in the housing to push the pin back down into the cylinder.

6. Starting with the pin farthest inside the cylinder, use the pick to push it up until you hear a click. That sound means that the pin has pushed an upper pin out of the cylinder and the slight pressure you have been applying to the tension wrench has misaligned the hole in

the housing with the hole in the cylinder, preventing the upper pin from falling back into the cylinder. The click is the sound of the upper pin falling back down on top of the cylinder. The lower pin falls back into the cylinder, but it is no longer held in place by the spring and upper pin in the housing.

7. Patiently repeat this process with all of the pins to push all the upper pins out of the cylinder.

8. Use the tension wrench to turn the cylinder and open the lock.

HOW IT WORKS

With a pin-and-tumbler lock, pairs of pins hold the cylinder in place. Pushing up the pins so they no longer prevent the cylinder from rotating allows you to turn the tumbler, opening the lock.

TAKE YOUR PICK

- If you don't have two bobby pins, you can use paper clips to pick a lock in the same basic manner described above.
- Using lock-picking tools to commit a crime is a felony.
- A successful lock picker understands the mechanics of how the parts of a lock work in harmony and how to exploit defects in that mechanism.
- A professional lock-picking set, containing a tension wrench and a pick, can be purchased through any locksmith tool company.
- Dental picks and craft picks also can be used to successfully pick a lock.
- Renowned magician Harry Houdini mastered the art of lock picking and owned a variety of lock picks, some of which folded up like a pocketknife, enabling him to open padlocks, handcuffs, and door locks.
- The five burglars arrested for breaking into the Democratic Party's offices in the Watergate building in 1972 possessed wiretapping, photographic, and lock-picking gear.

The All-Purpose Bobby Pin

Aside from holding your hair in place, the bobby pin has a variety of alternative uses.

- **Belt Clasp.** When wearing a lengthy belt around your waist, attach the extra-long belt flap back to the belt with a bobby pin.
- **Bookmark.** A bobby pin makes a simple, convenient bookmark.
- **Cherry or Olive Pitter.** Spread the legs of the bobby pin slightly, and then push the bobby pin through a cherry or olive to remove the pit.
- **Chip Clip.** Use a bobby pin to seal a potato chip bag closed.
- **Christmas Ornament Pin.** Insert the loop on a Christmas tree ornament through a bobby pin, and then clip the bobby pin to a branch of the tree to hang the ornament.
- **Clothespin.** In a pinch, you can use bobby pins as clothespins to attach lightweight clothes to a clothesline.
- **Function Button Activator.** Use the end of a bobby pin to press the tiny reset buttons in electronic devices.
- **Nail Art Tool.** Dip the tips of a bobby pin in nail polish to paint polka dots on your fingernails.
- **Nail Holder.** To avoid hammering your fingers by accident, use a bobby pin to hold a nail in place.
- **Safety Seal Opener.** Use a bobby pin to pop open the safety seals in food jars or medication bottles.
- **Tape Marker.** Mark the end of a roll of clear tape by adhering the bobby pin to the sticky side of the loose end.
- **Toothpaste Squeezer.** Clip a bobby pin along the width of the bottom of your toothpaste tube, and slide it up the tube to push the unused toothpaste to the top of the tube.
- **Yarn Ball Lock.** Clip the end of yarn ball string to the ball.
- **Zipper Tab.** If you lose a zipper tab, loop a bobby pin through the hole in the slider body.

How to Start a Campfire with Potato Chips

WHAT YOU NEED

- Bag of potato chips
- Small twigs and larger sticks
- Matches or butane lighter

WHAT TO DO

1. Open a bag of potato chips and pour a pile of chips wherever you wish to start a campfire.
2. Place twigs over the potato chips in a stack, leaving enough space for air to get between the twigs.
3. Stack larger sticks above the twigs.
4. Using a butane lighter or matches, light the potato chips on fire.

HOW IT WORKS

The potato chips, saturated with oil and kept dry in a Mylar bag, burn long enough and strong enough as tinder that even damp firewood will dry and catch fire before they burn out.

ALL FIRED UP

- In a pinch, you can use pencil shavings as tinder. Carrying a small pencil sharpener in your emergency kit enables you to make tinder on the spot. Simply sharpen a pencil or a small stick of wood. For wet wood, scrape off the soggy bark and then sharpen the remaining stick, making shavings from the dry interior.

- Store wooden matches in a clean, empty plastic prescription pill bottle. The waterproof canister keeps the matches secure and dry. If you're storing wooden matches, be sure to remove a striker from a matchbook or matchbox and slip it inside the canister as well. Even if you're stashing strike-anywhere matches in the canister, a striker stored in a waterproof canister may come in handy if you're soaking wet or stranded in a drenched area.

- You can also store matches or tinder inside a condom, which doubles as a waterproof container.

- To prevent the fuel lever on a butane lighter stored in a survival kit from accidentally being activated, emptying all the butane from the lighter, wrap a small zip tie around the body of the lighter and the fuel lever. When you're ready to use the lighter, simply clip off the zip tie.

- On November 8, 1991, two men and a woman started a fire at a 7-Eleven convenience store in Fort Lauderdale, Florida, that caused $250,000 worth of damage by jokingly burning a bag of potato chips. One of the men used a butane lighter to set fire to a bag of chips. The threesome laughed, tapped out the flames, bought some beer, and left. The smoldering chips reignited.

- At noon on May 28, 2013, a five-alarm fire broke out in the potato chip aisle of the Durango Supermercado grocery store in a Chicago suburb. When the smoke alarm sounded and store manager Jose Rivera went to investigate, he discovered the potato chip aisle was on fire and the chips were burning. He tried to put out the fire with an extinguisher, instructed costumers to leave the building, and returned to find the fire worsening and nothing left in the extinguisher. The blaze burned through the roof, causing a partial collapse of the building. Firefighters put out the blaze within the hour, and no injuries were reported.

How to Improvise Shoes with Rubber Gloves

WHAT YOU NEED

- Clean, empty cereal box
- Scissors
- Pencil or pen
- Rubber gloves
- Duct tape (optional)

WHAT TO DO

1. To improvise a pair of shoes in an emergency, use scissors to cut open the sides of the cereal box, creating a flat sheet of cardboard.

2. Place your bare feet on the cardboard and trace around them with the pencil or pen.

3. Cut out the footpads from the cardboard.

4. Wearing socks (if possible), insert each foot into a rubber glove with the thumb of the glove facing upward (rather than under the sole of your foot).

5. Slide the cardboard footpads into the glove under your sock or bare foot, to create an insole.

6. If desired, fold the fingers of the glove back toward the top of your foot and secure them to the rubber glove using duct tape.

7. If necessary, you can also run a strip of duct tape around the cuff of the glove to secure it to your ankle.

8. To reinforce the soles, apply strips of duct tape on the bottom of each shoe.

9. If the gloves do not fit on your feet (or if you desire a two-ply rubber sole), put on a pair of socks, flatten each glove, hold each glove to the sole of one foot, and secure it in place with duct tape.

HOW IT WORKS

The rubber glove doubles as a thick, impermeable sock that protects your feet, and the cardboard insole provides additional cushioning.

FITS LIKE A GLOVE

- Rather than throwing out a used pair of rubber gloves, use a pair of scissors to cut 1-inch-thick cuffs from the sleeve, creating a variety of giant rubber bands. Cut off the fingers from the glove and slip them onto the end of broom handles to  prevent the brooms from falling over when leaned against a wall (or making marks on the wall).
- To dry wet shoes or sneakers, crumple up several pages of a newspaper, shove the wads inside the wet shoes or sneakers, and let sit. When the newsprint becomes damp, change the paper. The newsprint absorbs excess water from the shoes or sneakers, speeding up the drying process.
- In the television series *Mad Men* (season 4, episode 11, "Chinese Wall"), advertising copywriter Peggy Olson pitches highly suggestive copy to promote Playtex gloves: "Playtex gloves protect a woman's hands, so they're soft enough to touch all the things a woman wants to touch."

How to Make Stilts with Plastic Paint Buckets

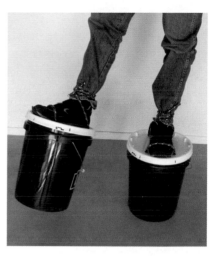

WHAT YOU NEED

- 2 plastic 5-gallon paint buckets with lids
- Indelible marker or pencil
- Ruler
- Drill with ½-inch bit
- 2 lengths of rope, 4 feet each
- Contact cement (optional)
- 2 clean, used mouse pads (optional)

WHAT TO DO

1. Trace the outline of one of your shoes or sneakers on top of one of the plastic paint bucket lids with the marker or pencil.

2. Make a mark on both sides of the shoe outline, roughly four inches from the toe, to indicate where the straps will be attached.

3. Make a mark on both sides of the shoe outline on both sides of the heel, to indicate where the heel straps will be attached.

4. Repeat steps 1 through 3 above with the other shoe and the second plastic paint bucket lid.

5. Snap the lids onto the paint buckets and drill ½-inch holes through the four marks you made on each lid.

6. For each lid, thread a 4-foot length of rope through the four holes in each lid to strap in the shoe over the toes and then wrap the rope around your ankles.

7. To prevent the paint bucket stilts from sliding on slippery floors, glue a clean, used mouse pad to the bottom of each bucket (optional).

8. Snap the lids onto the paint buckets and stand on the lids. Slip the toes of your shoes under the front rope and wrap the two long straps around your ankles.

HOW IT WORKS

Wearing the paint buckets on your feet makes you 18 inches taller, the width of the plastic buckets keeps you balanced, and the homemade stilts allow you to walk freely and easily. When you're not using the buckets as stilts, you can store tools or other objects in the empty buckets.

A DROP IN THE BUCKET

If you want to make more precise straps, simply drill ¼-inch holes at the marks and, using bolts, washers, and nuts, secure Velcro straps to the lids through the appropriate holes (two shorter straps alongside each foot and the two longer straps behind each heel). Painting expert Brian Santos, author of *Painting Secrets*, designed Velcro strap make-'em-yourself bucket stilts for painting ceilings and reaching tall walls.

How to Create Boots with Duct Tape

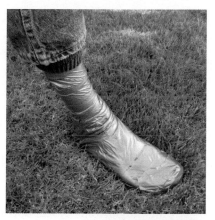

WHAT YOU NEED

- Pair of thick socks (or 2 pairs of thin socks)
- Flip-flops or sandals
- Duct tape

WHAT TO DO

1. To make boots in an emergency, put the socks on your feet.
2. While wearing the socks, put the flip-flops or sandals on your feet.

3. Wrap a 10-inch strip of duct tape around the sock and flip-flop on one foot, securing the sock and flip-flop together, but not too tightly. Give your foot some room to breathe.
4. Continue wrapping 10-inch strips of duct tape around the sock and flip-flop until you have created a boot and completely covered the sock.
5. Repeat with the second foot.

HOW IT WORKS

Wrapped around the sock and flip-flop, the duct tape creates a waterproof seal and protective coating.

TOO BIG FOR YOUR BOOTS

- The thicker the socks, the more cushioning and insulation they provide for these impromptu boots.
- If you do not have flip-flops, you can create boots by using a pair of socks and duct tape alone. Simply cover the bottom of the socks with several strips of duct tape to create a firm sole and then wrap the entire sock with duct tape.
- When you're finished wearing the boots, cut them off with a pair of surgical scissors (or safety scissors, with rounded tips), cutting straight down the front of the sock to the top of the foot.
- In her book *Wild*, author Cheryl Strayed describes making a pair of hiking boots from socks, sandals, and duct tape.

- To prevent your feet from getting blisters, before putting on the socks and wrapping them in duct tape, turn them inside out and rub a bar of soap on the inside of the sock at the heel and toes. The soap creates a smoother surface.

- To prevent trench foot (an injury caused by exposure to the cold and wet, causing the feet and toes to appear pale and feel cold and numb), do not wear the duct tape boots for more than 24 hours. If your feet get damp inside the boots from perspiration, continually wriggle your toes and bend your ankles to keep the blood circulating.

- To make a pair of flip-flops from two empty 2-liter soda bottles, use a pair of scissors to cut off the bottoms of the bottles. Flatten the bottles to form soles, cut three holes through each plastic sole (just like the holes in a regular pair of flip-flops), and thread and knot cord through the holes.

How to Write a Secret Message with Soap

WHAT YOU NEED

- Bar of soap, liquid hand soap, dishwashing soap, or shaving cream
- Wall mirror in a bathroom equipped with a shower
- Paper cup or drinking glass
- Cotton swab

WHAT TO DO

1. Using a bar of soap like a large piece of chalk, write your message on the mirror, making sure to press lightly so the message remains invisible.

2. If you don't have a bar of soap, put a couple of drops of liquid hand soap, dishwashing soap, or shaving cream in a paper cup or drinking glass, add some water, and use a cotton swab (or your finger) dipped in the solution to write your message on the mirror. Paint a thin coat of soap on the mirror so the message remains invisible.

HOW IT WORKS

When someone takes a shower in the bathroom with the door closed, the steam will condense on the mirror, except where the soap is   revealing your message. The soap marks on the mirror break up the surface tension of the water, preventing the words written on the mirror from fogging up with steam.

GET THE MESSAGE?

- In 500 BC, the ancient Greek tyrant Histiaeus wrote a secret message on the shaved head of a slave, waited for his hair to grow back, and then sent the slave across enemy lines. When the slave's head was shaved, the message was revealed.

- A message in invisible ink, written beneath a one-sentence love letter on a postcard sent from Poland in 1943, vividly describes the horrific conditions in a Nazi death camp and makes an urgent request for supplies. The postcard is on display at the Yad Vashem Holocaust Museum in Jerusalem.

How to Hide Valuables in a Tennis Ball, Deodorant Stick, or Tampon

TENNIS BALL

WHAT YOU NEED

- Single-edge razor blade, hobby knife, or sharp kitchen knife
- Tennis ball

WHAT TO DO

1. Using a single-edge razor blade, hobby knife, or sharp kitchen knife, carefully slice open the tennis ball approximately 4 inches along the seam.
2. Squeeze the ball, revealing the hollow cavity inside the ball.
3. Insert your valuables inside the ball.
4. Release the ball, allowing the rubber ball to spring back to its original shape and conceal the slit you cut into it.

DEODORANT STICK

WHAT YOU NEED

- Deodorant stick

WHAT TO DO

1. Remove the lid from the plastic canister.
2. Turn the plastic dial on the bottom of the canister to completely remove the deodorant stick from the canister.

3. Place your valuables inside the hollow plastic canister.
4. Replace the deodorant stick (or discard if preferred).
5. Replace the lid.

TAMPON

WHAT YOU NEED
- Box of tampons
- Scissors

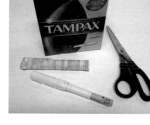

WHAT TO DO
1. Remove one tampon from the box.
2. Using a pair of scissors, gently cut open the end of the wrapper.
3. Slide the tampon out from the wrapper.
4. Roll up your money tightly and insert it into the hollow end of the cardboard applicator.
5. Place the tampon back in the wrapper and back in the box.

HOW IT WORKS
Tennis balls are hollow rubber balls, which, after being cut open, return to their original shape. Deodorant sticks are housed in hollow plastic canisters. Tampons are packaged in cardboard applicators, which are hollow at one end.

COLD CASH
Crime prevention experts suggest storing valuables or money in the freezer, a spot that burglars are less likely to ransack.

EVERY TRICK IN THE BOOK
A Fool and His Money

What are other good places to hide money around your home?

- **Curtain Rods.** Remove the decorative finial from one end of a curtain rod, roll up the bills, and insert them into the hollow rod. Then replace the decorative finial.
- **Drop Ceiling Tiles.** Slide open a ceiling tile in a drop ceiling, place a small bag or box of money or valuables atop the tile, and place the ceiling tile back in position.
- **Lip Balm Tubes.** Clean out an empty lip balm tube, roll up some bills, insert them into the tube, and replace the cap.
- **Picture Frames.** Remove the back from a picture frame, place several bills flat between the picture and the cardboard backing, and replace the back of the picture frame. Crooks rarely steal framed pictures of family and friends.
- **Soap Box.** An empty box that once contained a bar of soap is an excellent way to stash valuables among your bathroom supplies.

- **Soup Cans.** A can opener that cuts on the side of the can, just below the edge of the lid, allows you to reseal the lid on the can to store food. Using a side can opener, remove the top from a soup can, consume the contents, and then rinse the can and dry it thoroughly. Place money or valuables inside the can, replace the lid so it fits snugly, and hide the money safely among your canned goods.
- **Toys.** Unscrew the lid of the battery compartment of a broken toy, fit the folded bills inside, and screw the lid back on tightly.

- **Vacuum Cleaners.** Detach the cover as if you were going to replace the paper vacuum bag, stash your money behind the vacuum bag, and reattach the cover.
- **Vases.** Hide a ziplock bag filled with cash in the bottom of an opaque vase filled with fake flowers.

How to Make a Safe with a Hardcover Book

WHAT YOU NEED

- Hardcover book (1 inch or 2 inches thick)
- 2 binder clips
- Ruler
- Pencil
- Utility knife, hobby knife, or single-edge razor blade

- White glue (optional)
- Paintbrush (optional)
- Sheet of plastic wrap (optional)
- 8-inch-by-10-inch sheet of felt (optional)

WHAT TO DO

1. Open the book to page 11 and use the two binder clips to hold the first 10 pages to the front cover.

2. Using a ruler and pencil, measure and draw margins 1 inch wide on page 11, forming a rectangular frame on the page.

3. Using a utility knife, hobby knife, or single-edge razor blade (and the ruler as a straight-edge guide), cut along the rectangular frame roughly ¼ inch deep. Remove those cut pieces from the book to create a secret compartment.

4. Using the sides of the cutout as a template, continue cutting along the rectangular frame until you reach the last 10 to 20 pages of the book.

5. If you want to prevent the pages of your book safe from separating, apply a few coats of white glue with a paintbrush to the four inside edges of the rectangular cutout. Place a sheet of plastic wrap across the top of page 11 (to prevent the glue from adhering to the front pages), close the book, and place a few heavy books on top of the book to press the cutout pages together, allowing 24 hours for the glue to dry.

6. To give the book safe a touch of class, glue a sheet of felt inside the secret compartment.

7. Place money or valuables inside the cutout book, close the cover, and put the book on a bookshelf between books of a similar height, thickness, and subject matter.

HOW IT WORKS

A hollowed-out book makes an ideal place to hide valuables, giving you the perfect secondary use for that chemistry textbook you intended to throw out. The book itself is easily camouflaged on a bookshelf by the other books.

ONE FOR THE BOOKS

In 1980, Unabomber Ted Kaczynski mailed a package containing a pipe bomb hidden inside a hollowed book to United Airlines president Percy Wood. When Wood opened the book, the bomb exploded, injuring the executive.

EVERY TRICK IN THE BOOK
On the Same Page

Hollywood loves hiding things in books.

- *Escape from Alcatraz* **(1979).** Inmate Frank Morris (Clint Eastwood) hides a nail trimmer in a hollowed Bible.
- *From Russia with Love* **(1963).** In this James Bond movie, assassin Red Grant keeps a gun hidden in a hollowed copy of *War and Peace* by Leo Tolstoy.
- *The Game* **(1997).** Nicholas Van Orton (Michael Douglas) retrieves a gun from a hollowed-out copy of *To Kill a Mockingbird* by Harper Lee.
- *House* **(2006).** In season 3, episode 9 ("Finding Judas"), Dr. Gregory House (Hugh Laurie) hides a bottle of Vicodin in a hollowed textbook on lupus.
- *Lost* **(2005).** In season 2, episode 9 ("What Kate Did"), Eko (Adewale Akinnuoye-Agbaje) discovers a hollowed Bible that contains a small reel of film, which turns out to be the missing footage from the Dharma Initiative orientation film.
- *The Shawshank Redemption* **(1994).** Andy Dufresne (Tim Robbins) hides a small rock hammer in a cutout Bible. The pages are cut in the shape of the hammer.
- *The Three Musketeers* **(1993).** In this Disney movie, Aramis (Charlie Sheen) retrieves a pistol from a hollowed Bible.

How to Build a Wall Safe with an Electrical Socket

WHAT YOU NEED

- Drill with ¼-inch bit
- 8-inch length of stiff wire (or a wire clothes hanger)
- Plastic cut-in electrical box
- Pencil
- Drywall saw
- Screwdriver
- 120-volt duplex receptacle with two standard electrical sockets
- Faceplate with screw

WHAT TO DO

1. Choose a spot on the wall where you wish to locate your safe (the same height from the floor as existing receptacle boxes).

2. To make sure existing studs, joists, or pipes inside the wall will not obstruct the box, drill a small hole in the wall where you intend to locate the box. Bend the 8-inch length of wire in half to form a 90-degree angle, insert the wire into the hole, and turn it full circle. If you hit anything, drill another test hole a few inches to the left or right.

3. Hold the plastic cut-in electrical box against the wall and, using the pencil, trace around the box to create an outline of the box on the wall.

4. Drill a starter hole in one corner of the box drawn on the wall and use a drywall saw to cut out the rectangular hole.

5. Insert the plastic cut-in box into the hole and, using a screwdriver, tighten the clamp screws on the box to secure the box to the wall.

6. Place your money or valuables inside the plastic box embedded in the wall.

7. Use the screwdriver to attach the duplex receptacle to the box (with the two included screws, one at the top and one at the bottom of the receptacle).

8. Screw the faceplate onto the receptacle.

HOW IT WORKS

You've just installed a dummy electrical outlet. Since the outlet is not wired to your home's electrical system in any way, you can't get an electrical shock from the dummy outlet, nor can you power any lamps or electrical appliances with it. To access your money or valuables, use a screwdriver to detach the faceplate and the receptacle.

EVERYBODY'S GOT SOMETHING TO HIDE

- *Never attempt to hide money or valuables in a wired electrical outlet.* Doing so can trigger an electrical fire.
- In an episode of the television series *Breaking Bad* (season 5, episode 2, "Madrigal"), Walter White (Bryan Cranston) hides a ricin capsule behind an electrical outlet cover in his bedroom.
- On July 3, 2013, police in Aurora, Illinois, arrested a man who stashed marijuana inside an unused electrical outlet at the Aurora Rehabilitation & Living Center.

How to Cook Food with a Clothes Iron

WHAT YOU NEED

- Clothes iron
- 2 bricks

WHAT TO DO

Sunny-Side Up Eggs: Turn a clothes iron upside down, positioned between two bricks to keep the ironing surface level. Set the iron on heat with the steam setting turned off. Melt a slice of butter on the metal surface, then crack open an egg on the metal surface and, using a spatula, fry the egg.

Toast: To make toast using an iron, preheat the iron to the wool setting with the steam setting turned off, place a slice of bread on a wooden cutting board, and iron for 20 seconds.

Grilled Cheese Sandwich: Preheat the iron to the wool setting with the steam setting turned off, place a Kraft Single between two slices of Wonder Bread, place the sandwich on a wooden cutting board, and gently iron the top piece of bread for 20 seconds. Flip over the sandwich and iron for another 20 seconds.

HOW IT WORKS

The soleplate of the iron doubles as a cooking grill, heating to temperatures suitable for cooking.

IRON TEMPERATURES

The iron's adjustable dial indicates the multiple temperature control settings for different types of fabric and can be used to adjust the temperature for cooking. While irons made by various manufacturers tend to differ slightly in temperature, here are the approximate temperatures of common fabric settings.

- Linen: 445°F
- Cotton: 400°F
- Wool: 300°F
- Polyester: 300°F

- Silk: 300°F
- Acrylic: 275°F
- Nylon: 275°F

CLEANING

To clean the iron after cooking, set the iron on a steam setting, let it steam for 5 minutes, and then unplug it and let it cool. To clean any gunked-up residue from the soleplate of the iron, make a paste from baking soda and water and use a sponge to rub the paste onto the soleplate of the cool, unplugged iron. Rinse and dry.

COOK WHILE THE IRON IS HOT

- In 1882, Henry W. Weely invented the first electric iron. When plugged into its stand, the iron heated up. While being used, the iron cooled down rapidly, requiring the user to continually reheat the iron.
- Steam irons, first introduced in 1926, did not catch on until the late 1940s, when clothing makers introduced synthetic fabrics that scorched easily under a hot iron. To sell more irons, steam iron manufacturers began increasing the number of steam holes as a competitive marketing gimmick. The number of holes in the bottom of a steam iron slowly escalated from eight large holes to seventy small holes—in what industry insiders called a "holey war."
- In his 1957 novel *On the Road*, Jack Kerouac describes heating up a can of pork and beans with a clothes iron: "We found a nightclub singer in her hotel room who turned an iron upside down on a coat hanger in the wastebasket and warmed up a can of pork and beans."
- In the 1993 film *Benny & Joon*, Johnny Depp cooks a stack of grilled cheese sandwiches using a clothes iron.
- In an emergency, you can heat up a frozen TV dinner on the manifold of a running car engine. Make sure the car is in park with the parking brake set. Wrap the aluminum tray in a sheet of aluminum foil, set it on top of the manifold, and run the engine for 30 minutes.

EVERY TRICK IN THE BOOK
Spur-of-the-Moment Kitchenware

Eating can be a challenge without the proper utensils or dishware—unless you're willing to get creative.

- **Bowls.** To improvise a bowl, cut off the bottom of a clean, empty plastic 1- or 2-liter soda bottle to an appropriate height. If desired, use an emery board or a small piece of sandpaper to smooth the rough edge of the bottle.
- **Chopsticks.** From a tree, cut off two straight branches roughly the thickness and length of a pencil and use a pocketknife to whittle off the bark.
- **Containers.** Clean, empty plastic butter or margarine tubs make excellent bowls or storage containers.
- **Cups.** Cut off the bottom 3 inches from a waxed cardboard milk carton to create a drinking cup.
- **Dishware.** In an emergency, you can shape a sheet of aluminum foil into a bowl, cup, or plates.
- **Funnels.** To devise a funnel, cut the bottom off a clean, empty soda bottle, turn the upper half upside down, and remove the cap. Or, using a pair of scissors, snip off one of the bottom corners from a ziplock storage bag.
- **Glasses.** A clean, empty yogurt container makes an excellent measuring cup or drinking glass.
- **Mixing Bowl.** If you don't have a mixing bowl, pour all the ingredients into a ziplock storage bag, zip it shut, and then shake or knead the contents.
- **Paper Plate Holders.** To add support to a paper plates, place the paper plate inside an upside-down Frisbee.

How to Brew Coffee Without a Coffee Maker

WHAT YOU NEED

- Paintbrush
- Black paint
- Clean, empty coffee can with lid
- Aluminum foil
- Styrofoam cup or cardboard coffee cup
- Chopstick, scissors, or knife
- Coffee filter or sheet of paper towel
- 1 tablespoon of fresh coffee grounds
- Coffee mug

WHAT TO DO

1. Paint the outside of the coffee can and the top of the lid black.
2. Set the can on a sheet of aluminum foil outside in direct sunlight.
3. Fill the can with water and cover with the black lid.
4. Let the sealed can of water sit undisturbed for 1 hour, giving the sunlight enough time to heat up the water in the can.
5. Using the chopstick, scissors, or knife, punch four small holes in the bottom of the Styrofoam cup or cardboard coffee cup.
6. Line the inside of the cup with a coffee filter or a sheet of paper towel, and add 1 tablespoon of coffee grounds.
7. Hold the cup directly above a coffee mug, fill the cup with the hot water from the coffee can, and wait for the water to drip through the holes into the coffee mug, making precisely one cup of coffee.

HOW IT WORKS

The aluminum foil reflects sunlight toward the coffee can, which, painted black, converts light energy into heat energy, slowly heating the water inside the can to a maximum temperature of 300°F. Water boils at 212°F. Pouring water heated to 200°F over ground coffee beans extracts the oil from the beans. The coffee filter (or paper towel) catches the loose grounds and eliminates sediment as the liquid coffee drips through the holes in the bottom of the cup.

3

FOILED AGAIN

A terrorist attempts to hijack your plane. A bank robber takes you hostage. A gangster holds a gun to your head. With a little ingenuity and a dash of bravado you can incapacitate an assailant with something as simple as your keys, a sock, and a dead cell phone, or a can of aerosol deodorant.

How to Thwart a Terrorist with a Cell Phone

WHAT YOU NEED
- Sock or panty hose
- Cell phone

WHAT TO DO
1. Take off one sock or a pair of panty hose.
2. Slip the cell phone inside the foot of the sock or panty hose leg.
3. Clasping the open end of the sock or the knee of the panty hose leg, whirl it over your head like a lasso, swinging it around as fast as possible.
4. Without inadvertently hitting yourself, use the improvised weapon to strike the terrorist in the head. Or release the whirling sock, hurling the cell phone at the evildoer's head.

HOW IT WORKS
The sock and cell phone become a sling, which, when whirled above the head, can be hurled with more force than a person can deliver by throwing the objects.

BUSY SIGNALS
- If you don't have a cell phone accessible, place an unopened soda can or a bar of soap inside the sock (or a brick inside a pillowcase), creating a similar weapon.
- In the Bible, David slays Goliath with a stone hurled from a sling (I Samuel 17: 48–50).
- In ancient times, soldiers in the Egyptian, Greek, and Roman armies utilized slings in warfare.
- If you hurl your cell phone and miss your target, you can use the cord on the earbud headphones to strangle the terrorist. Wrap the ends of the cord around your hands, wrap the cord around the terrorist's neck from behind, place your knee against the enemy's back, and pull with all your might. Strangulation compresses the carotid arteries, which carry blood to the brain, typically inducing unconsciousness within 15 seconds.
- If you have neither a cell phone nor earbud headphones, you can always strangle a terrorist with a necktie.

How to Slip Up an Attacker with Dishwashing Liquid

WHAT YOU NEED
- Dishwashing liquid
- Water
- Bucket
- Mop

WHAT TO DO
1. To make a tile floor excessively slippery to trip up an attacker, mix ¼ cup of dishwashing liquid in 1 gallon of water in a bucket.
2. Pour the solution on the floor.
3. If time permits, carefully spread the puddle with a mop.

HOW IT WORKS
The soapy solution reduces the floor's coefficient of friction, causing the shoes of anyone who attempts to cross the floor to lose traction. The shoes slip out from under the person, causing that individual to fall to the ground—just like a person falling on ice.

WARNING
Intentionally making a floor slippery and causing a person to fall, break a hip bone, suffer a concussion, wind up paralyzed for life, or die—could make you liable for premeditated murder or other serious charges.

GIVING 'EM THE SLIP
- If you don't have any dishwashing liquid, add a few teaspoons of baby oil or vegetable oil to a bucket of water, and pour that solution across the floor. The oil molecules spread out in a thin film on the surface of the water spill, creating an incredibly slippery oil slick.
- You can also grease up a floor with a coat of vegetable shortening or furniture polish.
- On March 5, 2011, a pair of robbers entered Tatiana's Hair Salon in Rochester, New York, brandished handguns, and demanded cash from the hairstylist and her customers. Then both men slipped and fell on the linoleum floor, stood back up, and fled the salon.
- A business owner or employee who mops a slippery floor and fails to put up a WET FLOOR sign could be guilty of negligence.

How to Create an Oil Slick with Vegetable Oil

WHAT YOU NEED
- 1 cup of vegetable oil
- Clean, empty 1-gallon bleach jug with cap
- Water

WHAT TO DO
1. Pour 1 cup of vegetable oil into the clean, empty bleach jug.
2. Fill the rest of the bottle with water.
3. Replace the cap on the bottle, secured tightly, and store the bottle in the trunk of your car.
4. If you find yourself being pursued by a villain in a car, put enough distance between you and your predator to give yourself sufficient time to park the car by the side of the road, retrieve the prepared bottle from your trunk, and pour the oily solution across the lane of the road to form a puddle.
5. Get back in your car and flee the scene.

HOW IT WORKS
The oil in the puddle of water spreads out in a thin film across the entire puddle, forming an oil slick. A car hydroplanes on the oil-slick asphalt, causing the tires to skid. The driver then loses control of the vehicle and veers off the road.

WARNING
Intentionally creating an oil slick that causes a car to skid off the road and kill someone could make you liable for premeditated murder.

HIT THE ROAD
- In the 1964 movie *Goldfinger*, James Bond (Sean Connery) presses a button in his Aston Martin DB5 sports car to release an oil slick.
- To regain control of a car if you go into a skid, do not hit the brakes. Instead, gently turn the wheels into the skid. If the wheels start to skid in the other direction, gently turn the wheels in that direction. When you feel the steering wheel regain control of the road, straighten the wheel to bring the vehicle back into the middle of your lane.

How to Blind an Evildoer with Cayenne Pepper

WHAT YOU NEED

- Rubber gloves
- Safety glasses
- Dust mask (or bandana)
- Funnel
- 8 tablespoons of cayenne pepper
- 12 ounces of isopropyl rubbing alcohol (or white vinegar)
- 2 tablespoons of vegetable oil
- Clean, empty 1 or 2 liter soda bottle with cap
- Coffee filter (or sheet of paper towel)
- Clean, empty pump bottle with an adjustable nozzle (or trigger-spray bottle)

WHAT TO DO

1. Wearing the rubber gloves, safety glasses, and dust mask, use the funnel to pour the cayenne pepper, rubbing alcohol, and vegetable oil into the soda bottle.
2. Place the cap on the bottle, secure it tightly, and shake it well.
3. Let the bottle sit overnight in a cool place to let the solution mature, allowing the capsaicin (the active ingredient in cayenne pepper) to dissolve in the alcohol and vegetable oil, magnifying the intensity of the capsaicin.
4. Line the funnel with a coffee filter (or sheet of paper towel) and pour the strained solution into the pump bottle with an adjustable nozzle.
5. To incapacitate an assailant, do not extend your arm with the pump bottle pointed in the attacker's face. Doing so gives the assailant the opportunity to grab the pump bottle and use it against you. Instead, extend your free arm and yell, "Stop!" to distract the attacker. With the other hand, aim the nozzle of the pump bottle at your assailant's face, and when the attacker comes within range, fire a short burst of the homemade pepper spray.
6. Back up immediately to get away from the resultant fog and to flee from the attacker.

HOW IT WORKS

Cayenne pepper contains capsaicin, an alkaline oil that produces an agonizing burning sensation when it comes into contact with mucous membranes, irritating the eyes and causing temporary blindness. Capsaicin dissolves in alcohol, vinegar, and vegetable oil, spreading the compound's molecules equally throughout the liquid and maximizing the potency of the nonlethal capsaicin. The vegetable oil also helps the peppery liquid adhere to the body or clothes.

SPICE IT UP

- Stored in a sealed bottle, the homemade pepper spray, preserved by the alcohol or vinegar, remains potent up to three months.
- Never use pepper spray on food. Pepper spray issued to law enforcement officers contains 10 percent capsaicin, varying from 2 million to 6 million units on the Scoville scale, which rates the spicy heat of peppers. Store-bought pepper spray contains 2 to 10 percent capsaicin, varying from 500,000 to 2 million units. In contrast, the original red Tabasco Pepper Sauce scores between 2,500 and 5,000 units on the Scoville scale.
- Birds cannot taste cayenne pepper. To keep squirrels out of a bird feeder, sprinkle the birdseed with cayenne pepper. Unlike the birds, the squirrels can taste the pepper and want nothing to do with it.
- In a life-or-death situation, a can of wasp or hornet insecticide, sprayed in an assailant's eyes, causes temporary blindness. Be advised that the warning label on most canisters of aerosol insecticide states, *"It is a violation of federal law to use this product in a manner inconsistent with its labeling."* Wasp and hornet sprays contain pyrethrin, a toxin that can have dangerous effects and may be deemed illegal as a self-defense spray in many jurisdictions.

How to Disable a Car with Water

WHAT YOU NEED
- Plastic longneck watering can (with an elongated narrow neck)
- Water

WHAT TO DO
1. Fill the longneck watering can with water.
2. Open the metal gas tank flap on the car, unscrew the gas cap, and insert the elongated narrow neck of the plastic watering can into the hole leading to the gas tank.
3. Empty the water into the tank.
4. Remove the neck of the watering can from the gas tank.
5. Replace the gas cap securely and close the metal gas tank flap on the car.

HOW IT WORKS
Water, being heavier than gasoline, sinks to the bottom of the gas tank and gets drawn into the fuel line before the gas, causing the car engine to sputter and conk out (because water, unlike gasoline, is not combustible).

STEP ON IT!
- Contrary to popular belief, putting sugar in a gas tank does not disable a car immediately. Sugar does not dissolve in gasoline, so the sugar granules, sitting dormant at the bottom of the gas tank, cannot quickly travel through the fuel lines to clog the filters. Also, gasoline will not caramelize and turn the cylinders into a sticky mess because several filters between the tank and the engine will prevent the sugar from ever reaching the engine. However, the sugar will eventually clog up the fuel filter and stop the car from running, forcing the owner to replace the fuel filter several times to strain out the sugar.
- Water in the gas tank disables the car immediately, so be certain that you can get far away from your potential assailant before the burglar, robber, kidnapper, or terrorist tries to start the car.
- All underground gasoline tanks, such as those used by gas stations, accumulate water, which, being heavier than gasoline, settles to the bottom of the tank.

How to Improvise an Alarm System with a Mousetrap

WHAT YOU NEED

- Duct tape
- Mousetrap
- Dental floss (or fishing line)

WHAT TO DO

1. Using one strip of duct tape, adhere the mousetrap to the doorframe 5 inches above the floor. Position the mousetrap horizontally with the catch facing the doorway.
2. Tie a loop at the end of the dental floss.
3. Slip the loop over the copper holding bar and set the trap (with the loop running through the bar.
4. Carefully run the dental floss to the opposite doorframe (without springing the trap) and tape it in place.

HOW IT WORKS

When someone walks through the dental floss, the floss tugs the holding bar, releasing it and triggering the mousetrap to snap shut with a bang.

SHUT YOUR TRAP

- To make the mousetrap alarm sound louder, glue a few party snaps along the indentation in the mousetrap base where the metal bow hits the wood.
- The mousetrap alarm can also be rigged to trigger an electronic alarm or device. Attach one end of a wire to the end of the spring on the trap, and attach the other end of the wire to one terminal on a battery. Attach a second wire to a metal thumbtack, which you then press into the wooden base of the trap so that when the mousetrap is triggered, the metal bar snaps down on the thumbtack, making contact. Attach the opposite end of the second wire to one of the two terminals on a battery-powered bicycle horn or a flashlight bulb. Run a third wire from the second terminal on the battery to the second terminal on the bicycle horn or flashlight bulb.

How to Rig Up an Alarm System with Bang Snaps

WHAT YOU NEED
- 4 thumbtacks
- Sheet of paper towel
- 6 to 12 bang snaps

WHAT TO DO
1. Open the door you intend to alarm.
2. Use two thumbtacks to attach one edge of a sheet of paper towel to the center of the top side of a door, so that the paper towel hangs behind the open door.
3. Step inside the door and close it behind you.
4. Use the remaining two thumbtacks to attach the hanging end of the paper towel to the door frame above the door, creating a loop of paper towel on the inside of the door.
5. Insert a handful of bang snaps inside the loop of paper towel.
6. Do not open the door.

HOW IT WORKS
When someone opens the door, the paper towel will spring open, sending the bang snaps falling to the floor, where they will explode. (The action of opening the door will also rip the paper towel apart.)

SNAP TO IT
Bang snaps (also known as pop snaps, party snaps, and snappers) are small novelty fireworks made from a small quantity of sand mixed with approximately 0.08 mg of silver fulminate, wrapped in thin paper. When thrown against a hard surface, the bang snaps produce a loud bang—without a physical explosion.

How to Open a Padlock with a Soda Can

WHAT YOU NEED

- Tin snips (or sharp scissors)
- Clean, empty aluminum soda can
- Ruler
- Indelible marker
- Pen or round pencil

WHAT TO DO

1. Using tin snips, cut off the top and bottom of the aluminum soda can.
2. Cut a single vertical line through the can, creating one long sheet of aluminum.
3. With the ruler and indelible marker, draw a rectangle on the aluminum sheet measuring 2½ inches in length and 1¾ inch in height.

4. Cut out the rectangle, being careful not to cut yourself on the sharp aluminum.
5. With the ruler and marker, draw a line dividing the height of the rectangle in half.
6. Cut two triangles into the bottom half of the rectangle, making the rectangle look like the letter M. Round the bottom midpoint of the letter M.

7. Fold the top rectangle in half, bringing the top edge down to meet the tops of cutout triangles.

8. Fold the legs of the M up and over the flap you folded down in step 7, and wrap the entire length of the legs around that flap.
9. Wrap the completed shim around a pen or round pencil to curve the rounded triangle of aluminum enough so that it will slide into the shackle of a padlock.

10. Insert the curved, rounded triangle on the shim into the space between the padlock body and the shackle, on the side opposite the shackle's locking groove.

11. With the shim inserted into the shackle, turn the shim from side to side while tugging the shackle up and down—until the lock opens.

HOW IT WORKS

The rounded midpoint of the M in the aluminum shim allows you to wedge it well into the locking mechanism. Tugging the shackle up and down while turning the shim back and forth helps the shim move the locking mechanism out of the notch in the shackle, opening the lock.

LOCK, STOCK, AND BARREL

- Most padlocks provide only the illusion of security because they can be easily opened with a shim. While padlocks may not provide much protection against a determined thief, padlocks do help keep honest people honest.
- For do-gooders, knowing how to open a padlock with a homemade shim can be useful in an emergency situation—when someone forgets a combination, loses a key, or finds himself or herself padlocked in a cage.

How to Disable a Smoke Detector with Toothpaste

WHAT YOU NEED
- Tube of toothpaste

WHAT TO DO
1. Squeeze the toothpaste into the smoke detector vents.
2. Make sure you have sealed all the vents completely.

HOW IT WORKS
There are two main types of smoke detectors: ionization detectors and photoelectric detectors. Ionization detectors contain a minute quantity of americium-241 (perhaps $\frac{1}{5000}$ of a gram), which ionizes the oxygen and nitrogen atoms in the air in the chamber, generating a small, continuous electric current. Smoke entering the ionization chamber neutralizes the ions, breaking the circuit and triggering the alarm. In the most common photoelectric detectors, smoke particles scatter a beam of light onto a photocell, triggering the alarm. When the vents leading into a smoke detector are clogged with toothpaste, smoke cannot enter the chamber and trigger the alarm.

SMOKE AND MIRRORS
- If you don't have any toothpaste, you can disable a smoke detector with a shower cap by simply putting the plastic cap over the alarm. Or cover the smoke detector with a sheet of plastic wrap and secure it in place with a rubber band. Or, if the smoke detector isn't mounted to the wall or ceiling, simply remove the battery. Duh.
- Tampering with, disabling, or destroying the smoke detector in the lavatory aboard an airplane violates Federal Aviation Administration regulations and can result in a fine of up to $2,000.
- Disabling a smoke detector can expose you to legal and financial liability if a fire causes damage that could have been prevented had a working smoke detector sounded.

How to Break into a Locked Suitcase with a Ballpoint Pen

WHAT YOU NEED

- Ballpoint pen

WHAT TO DO

1. To get into a locked, zippered suitcase, jab the point of a ballpoint pen into the sealed zipper combs near the lock—puncturing the seal made by the zipper teeth.
2. With the pen inserted into the perforation between the zipper teeth, glide the pen along the zipper to open the suitcase.
3. To reseal the suitcase, simply grab the lock holding the zipper mechanism shut and zip up the suitcase.
4. Return the zipper mechanism to its original position, leaving no sign that anyone has tampered with the suitcase.

HOW IT WORKS

The zipper is a meshed-tooth slider fastener, and jabbing and sliding a sharp object between the fastened meshed teeth separates them, just like the mechanical slider does.

LIVING OUT OF A SUITCASE

- To help prevent a firearm or valuables from being stolen from a zippered suitcase, keep the items in a lockbox tethered inside the suitcase with a cable looped through the metal bars of the frame behind the liner.
- To make a stubborn zipper glide with greater ease, coat the teeth with lip balm, petroleum jelly, or vegetable shortening. Or rub a bar of soap or an unwrapped crayon along the teeth. Lubricating the teeth helps the zipper zip smoothly.

- To prevent a zipper from unzipping of its own accord, spray the teeth with hair spray or spray starch to give them greater traction.

How to Tie Up a Bad Guy with Panty Hose

WHAT YOU NEED

- Scissors or sharp knife
- Pair of panty hose

WHAT TO DO

1. With a pair of scissors or a sharp knife, cut off the legs from a pair of panty hose.

2. Squatting behind your subdued assailant, wrap one of the panty hose legs around the subject's ankles, from the back to front.

3. Cross the two ends in front of the ankle, pull tightly, and thread one end back between the ankles and under the back panty hose.

4. Pull tightly, bringing the feet and ankles together, and tie an overhand knot, followed by a second overhand knot and a third overhand knot.

5. When your knots are sturdy enough, tie a knot in each end of the panty hose leg, pulling each knot tight against the wad of knots to prevent your captive from wiggling them loose.

6. Seat your detainee in a standard upright chair and instruct him to place his arms behind the backrest of the chair, with his wrists together.

7. Wrap the second panty hose leg around the subject's wrists, from the back to front.

8. Cross the two ends in front of the wrist, pull tightly, and thread one end back between the wrists and under the back panty hose.

9. Pull tightly, bringing the palms and wrists together, and tie an overhand knot, followed by a second overhand knot, and a third overhand knot.

10. When your knots are sturdy enough, tie a knot in each end of the leg, slipping the knot tight against the wad of knots, to prevent your inmate from wiggling the knots loose.

11. To gag your prisoner, use the scissors or knife to cut open the remaining panty to create a long strip of nylon. Hold both ends of the strip and twirl it to roll up the nylon.

12. Standing behind the bound captive, wrap the middle of the nylon strip between his lips and around his head, knotting it several times behind his neck.

HOW IT WORKS

Panty hose legs, made from nylon and spandex, make a durable, strong substitute for rope.

TIED UP IN KNOTS

- In 1959, Glen Raven Mills of North Carolina introduced panty hose to the world, eventually developing a seamless model just in time for the advent of the miniskirt in 1965.

- In 1978, country music singer Tammy Wynette finished shopping at Nashville's Green Hills mall and returned to her car to find a man in the backseat holding a pistol and wearing panty hose over his face. The gunman ordered Wynette to drive, eventually dragged her into a field, tied a pair of panty hose around her neck, and punched her. Wynette played dead until the kidnapper fled the scene. The singer staggered up the road to a nearby house, where the residents cut the stocking from Wynette's neck. "She was gaspin' for breath, it was really tight," Junette Young told *People* magazine. "It was all I could do to get my finger between the panty hose and her neck."

- On October 11, 2003, passengers aboard an Aeroméxico flight from Mexico City to Paris helped flight attendants restrain 25-year-old Alexander Siess, who had been drinking heavily and disturbing passengers. Roughly a dozen passengers intervened, dragging Siess to the rear of the plane and tying him up with panty hose. The flight was diverted to New York's JFK Airport, but Siess was dead when the plane landed.

How to Make a Flame-Throwing Torch with Deodorant

WHAT YOU NEED
- Can of aerosol deodorant
- Butane lighter

WHAT TO DO
1. Stand outdoors in the middle of an empty area, with a can of aerosol deodorant in one hand and a butane lighter in the other.
2. With one hand, hold the butane lighter at arm's length directly in front of you and ignite it.
3. With the other hand, spray the can of deodorant—aimed away from you—over the flame.
4. When the stream of vapor catches fire, release the trigger mechanism on the butane lighter and lower that arm, but keep spraying the deodorant, which will continue burning with a bright flame up to 6 feet long.

HOW IT WORKS
The stream of vapor emitted from the aerosol can catches fire and continues burning, turning the deodorant can into a flamethrower.

FANNING THE FLAMES
- You can also make a flame-throwing torch with a can of aerosol hair spray. The hair spray, when sprayed into the air, becomes aerated, suspended in a flammable acetone solution.
- There is no air inside a can of aerosol hair spray or aerosol deodorant, so the flame cannot travel back inside the can and cause an explosion.
- On July 17, 1983, a family of seven Cuban refugees used a knife and an aerosol spray can converted into a torch to hijack Delta Airlines Flight 722 from Miami to Havana.
- In 2008, hundreds of protesters stormed the headquarters of Egypt's most prominent opposition politician, Ayman Nour, and set it on fire using aerosol cans to spray flames.

4

SECRET WEAPONS

You can fashion a weapon from almost anything—an old toothbrush, a ballpoint pen, or even an old bicycle inner tube. Or defend yourself in an emergency by improvising a stink bomb, smoke screen, or dart gun with everyday items you probably have in the house right now.

How to Make a Smoke Bomb with Sugar

WHAT YOU NEED

- ¼ cup of sugar
- 3 ounces of saltpeter (from a drugstore or medical supply store)
- Bowl
- Spoon
- Saucepan
- Paper cup
- Wooden matches

WHAT TO DO

1. Combine the sugar and saltpeter in the bowl.
2. Heat the mixture in the saucepan over very low heat, stirring constantly with the spoon, until the mixture melts into a plastic substance that resembles caramel.
3. Remove the mixture from the heat, poor it into the paper cup, embed a few wooden matches, heads up, into the hardening substance, and let it cool.
4. When the smoke bomb cools and hardens, peel off the paper cup, place the smoke bomb inside a clean, empty tin can or on a concrete surface (away from flammable objects or areas), light the match heads, and stand back. (Or you can simply leave the paper cup in place and light it on fire.)

HOW IT WORKS

Saltpeter (potassium nitrate), commonly used as a preserving and pickling salt in ancient Chinese kitchens, is one of the three original ingredients in fireworks. The melted sugar becomes a candy that encapsulates the saltpeter, making it easier to ignite.

UP IN SMOKE

On May 10, 2012, synchronized smoke-bomb attacks at multiple locations at the height of morning rush hour sent clouds of smoke billowing through the key transfer points in Montreal's subway system, cutting off service on every subway line for 90 minutes. Police arrested four suspects.

How to Create a Stink Bomb with Ammonia

WHAT YOU NEED

- Knife or single-edge razor blade
- Box of wooden safety matches
- Clean, empty glass jar with lid
- 1 cup of ammonia

WHAT TO DO

1. Use the knife or single-edge razor blade to carefully cut off the heads of 50 matches.
2. Place the match heads in the jar.
3. Add the ammonia to the jar and immediately screw the lid on tightly.
4. Let it sit for one week.
5. The solution can be thrown or poured directly into the target area. Or place the jar, uncapped, behind a door that opens into the target room. When someone enters, the door will knock over the jar, spilling the liquid, which smells like rotten eggs.

HOW IT WORKS

The sulfur in the match heads combines with the ammonia to form ammonium sulfide.

CREATING A STINK

The most vile-smelling substances in the world, according to *The Guinness Book of Records*, are ethyl mercaptan and butyl seleno mercaptan, each with a smell reminiscent of a combination of rotting cabbage, garlic, onions, burned toast, and sewer gas.

How to Create a Fireball with Flour

WHAT YOU NEED

- Drill with a ¼-inch bit
- Clean, empty coffee can with plastic lid
- Plastic tubing
- Scissors
- Electrical tape
- Candle (1-inch diameter)
- Matches
- 2 tablespoons of flour

WHAT TO DO

1. Drill a hole in the side of the coffee can, as close to the bottom rim as possible.
2. Insert 1 inch of the plastic tubing into the hole in the side of the can. Use the scissors to cut small pieces of electrical tape to seal the spaces between the tube and the hole in the can.
3. Using the scissors, cut off a 1-inch-tall piece of the candle, making sure to leave enough wick so you can light it later. Using the matches, light the bigger candle and carefully let 10 drops of hot wax drip to the center of the inside of the metal bottom of the coffee can. Secure the shorter candle upright inside the coffee can on the center of the bottom.

4. Outdoors, place 2 tablespoons of flour around the candle inside the coffee can. Carefully light the candle and cover the coffee can with the lid.
5. Blow hard into the free end of the plastic tube.

HOW IT WORKS

The plastic lid blows off the coffee can with a momentary blast of fire and smoke. When suspended in air, flour is highly flammable.

GREAT BALLS OF FIRE

- The fact that flour is highly flammable when suspended in air explains why explosions often occur in grain storage facilities.
- Most explosions from flour dust happen in grain elevators.
- If you don't have access to a plastic tube, use a garden hose.
- You can also create a fireball by throwing a handful of flour just above a lit candle.
- One of the first known dust cloud explosions took place in a flour mill in Turin, Italy, in 1785. No one realized for 100 years that the explosion had been initiated by ignition of the dust.
- In 1921, a dust explosion destroyed the largest grain elevator in the world, in Chicago, even though ignition hazards had been removed from the design to make the building fireproof.

How to Create a Molotov Cocktail with Tampons

WHAT YOU NEED

- Empty wine bottle
- Gasoline, turpentine, mineral spirits, acetone, rubbing alcohol, 80 proof liquor, or lamp oil
- Tampon
- Duct tape
- Butane lighter or matches

WHAT TO DO

1. Fill the wine bottle two-thirds full with gasoline, turpentine, mineral spirits, acetone, rubbing alcohol, 80 proof liquor, or lamp oil.
2. Unwrap the tampon, remove the applicator, and soak the tampon in whatever fuel you have used to fill the bottle.
3. Insert the tampon into the neck of the bottle (leaving the string and roughly half of the tampon sticking out of the mouth of the bottle) and secure the tampon in place with a piece of duct tape.
4. Using the butane lighter or matches, light the string on fire.
5. When the top of the tampon goes up in flames, hurl the bottle with the intent to break the glass.

HOW IT WORKS

The glass bottle breaks, spreading a large puddle of fuel, which immediately catches fire from the burning tampon.

TWO DOUCHEBAGS

- In 2008, police arrested David McKay and Bradley Crowder for possession of eight Molotov cocktails made from wine or liquor bottles, a mixture of gasoline and oil, and each with a tampon wick secured to its neck with rubber bands. McKay and Crowder had planned to hurl the firebombs at state-owned vehicles.
- On January 7, 2012, Pennsylvania police arrested a man and woman outside a bar in Metal Township for attempting to shove a lit tampon into the gas tank of a parked car.
- In the novel *Undertow* by Cherry Adair, Teal makes Molotov cocktails from empty bubble bath bottles and tampons.

How to Fashion a Slingshot from a Bicycle Inner Tube

WHAT YOU NEED

- Knife or saw
- Thick, forked branch (shaped like the letter Y)
- Scissors
- Bicycle inner tube
- Small stone, marble, or coin

WHAT TO DO

1. Using a knife or saw, carefully cut slots measuring 1¼ inches long in the ends of each fork of the Y-shaped branch.
2. Using scissors, cut a strip of bicycle inner tube 1½ inches wide by twice the length of the distance between the two forks of the Y-shaped branch.
3. Tie a knot in both ends of the long inner-tube strip.
4. Slip each end of the inner tube into a slot in the forks of the Y-shaped branch so that the knot holds the inner tube in place when you pull the inner tube.
5. Hold a stone in the center of the inner tube.
6. Pull back the projectile in the inner tube, stretching the rubber taut, aim, and release.

HOW IT WORKS

When the strip of rubber inner tube snaps back into its original shape, the force created by the tension hurls the projectile at a high speed.

SLINGS AND ARROWS

- To fashion a slingshot from a rubber glove, follow the directions above, substituting a rubber glove for the inner tube.
- A slingshot can be used for self-defense or, if you're foraging for food in the wilderness, to hunt birds, squirrels, or rabbits.

How to Build a Bola with Tennis Balls

WHAT YOU NEED

- Sharp knife or single-edge razor blade
- 3 or more tennis balls
- Scissors
- Rope
- Wire clothes hanger
- Masking tape
- Gravel, marbles, or spare coins
- Duct tape

WHAT TO DO

1. Using a sharp knife or single-edge razor blade, carefully cut two X-shaped holes into opposite sides of the tennis balls.
2. Using scissors, cut the rope into 3-foot lengths—one for each tennis ball.
3. Straighten the wire clothes hanger, tape the end of one length of rope to the end of the hanger, and thread the end of the rope through the two Xs in one of the tennis balls.
4. Remove the tape, withdraw the wire, and tie an overhand knot at the end of the rope so that the ball dangles at the end of the rope without falling off.
5. Using this same technique, thread a rope through each remaining tennis ball.

6. Fill each tennis ball with gravel, marbles, or spare coins—shoving the weights through the X-shaped holes.
7. Tie an overhand knot in each rope at the other end of the balls to securely anchor each ball at the end of its rope.
8. Wrap duct tape around each ball to secure it to the rope.
9. Knot the free ends of three (or more) ropes together and wrap duct tape around the knot to secure it.
10. Holding the end of the ropes knotted together, twirl the bola over your head and hurl it like a lasso at an assailant's legs.

HOW IT WORKS

A bola (Spanish for *ball*) is a throwing weapon with three weights tied to the ends of three ropes. When hurled at an adversary's legs, the bola quickly wraps around them, binding, tripping, and pounding the evildoer with one quick motion.

A WHOLE NEW BALL GAME

- Primitive peoples used the bola to hunt some 400,000 years ago.
- Gauchos in South America hunt with bolas consisting of two to three rawhide-covered balls filled with shot or iron. They use three-balled bolas for horses and two-balled bolas for ostrich and guanaco, which are bolaed around the neck.
- Another way to make a bola: Cut off three legs from two pairs of clean, used panty hose. Drop a bar of soap into the foot of each panty hose leg. Tie a knot in the foot to anchor each bar of soap in place, and knot the free ends of the three legs together.

How to Make a Knife from a Toothbrush

WHAT YOU NEED
- Toothbrush
- Rough concrete or brick surface
- Baby oil or water (optional)
- Duct tape (optional)

WHAT TO DO
1. Choose whichever end of the toothbrush will make the best knife blade. If the handle grip is thick rubber, choose the bristle end for the knife blade and remove the bristles (either by scraping them off, cutting them off, or using matches to melt them off).

2. Rub the toothbrush back and forth against a rough concrete or brick surface to file down the wide sides of the plastic to make the knife blade. Make the knife blade narrower near the tip of the toothbrush but thick enough to withstand breaking upon impact.  The finer the grit in the stone, the finer you can sharpen the blade. For best results, start off sharpening the knife on rough grit and finish on finer grit.

3. To sharpen the knife with greater precision, add a few drops of baby oil or water to the stone. The lubricant reduces the heat produced from the friction created by rubbing the plastic against the stone. Too much heat can warp the blade. Lubrication also helps clear away the debris generated by grinding the plastic against the stone.

4. To sharpen the blade, hold the edge of the knife against the stone at the angle you want to make the blade, then slowly stroke the knife along the stone while simultaneously pulling the knife back toward you (to sharpen the entire edge). Continue making long strokes along the entire edge, keeping the angle consistent.

5. If the plastic is sufficiently firm, create a spearhead at the end of the blade by filing the two narrow sides to a tapered point.

6. If the handle of the toothbrush is too slender to clasp properly in your hand, thicken the grip by wrapping it with several layers of duct tape.

7. To conceal the knife on your person, wear a long-sleeve shirt, slide the knife up the sleeve, and hold the handle with your palm.

HOW IT WORKS

The coarse concrete or brick surface works like sandpaper to grind down, smooth, and sharpen the plastic toothbrush.

LOOK SHARP!

- The word *shiv* is slang for "knife," and it refers to any sharp object used as a knife, including a razor blade, saw, or lawnmower blade.
- The slang word *shank* refers to a mundane object modified into a bladed or sharp-pointed weapon.
- To make a crude shank, fold a tin can lid in half, and make a handle by wrapping a strip of cloth around one end of the shank and securing the cloth in place with cord or wire.
- Prisoners have made shivs and shanks from spoons, combs, metal struts from bed frames, and shards of glass.

EVERY TRICK IN THE BOOK
Cut and Run

You can make knifelike weapons from a wide variety of objects.

- **Brooms or Mop Handles**. Sharpened like a spear.
- **Car Keys**. Gripped in your fist and placed so they protrude from between your fingers.
- **China Plates**. Broken with a jagged edge.
- **Credit Cards**. Cut diagonally in half.
- **Eyeglass Lenses**. Broken into shards of razor-sharp glass.
- **Fireplace Pokers**. Particularly when the end is heated in fire.
- **Metal Wristwatch Band**. Worn over the knuckles, it tears flesh when delivered to the face with a punch.

How to Make a Marble Gun with a Condom

WHAT YOU NEED
- Utility knife
- Clean, empty Gatorade bottle
- Condom (nonlubricated)
- Marbles

WHAT TO DO
1. Using a utility knife, carefully remove the label from a clean, empty Gatorade bottle and cut the bottom off the plastic bottle.
2. Unwrap the condom and secure the open end of the condom over the lip of the bottle.
3. Holding the plastic bottle, pull back the tip of the condom to make sure it stays secured to the bottle.
4. Holding the open end of the plastic bottle upright, drop a marble into the bottle and into the tip of the condom.
5. From the outside of the condom, hold the marble between your thumb and index finger, and aiming the open end of the plastic bottle at your target, pull the condom back like a slingshot.
6. Let go of the marble and condom, allowing the latex condom to snap back into place, shooting the marble up to 50 feet at high speeds.

HOW IT WORKS
The elastic condom shoots like a slingshot, and the plastic bottle imitates the barrel of a gun, steadying the shot and providing accuracy.

LOSING YOUR MARBLES
Instead of marbles, you can use this device to launch pennies, binder clips, paper clips, erasers, M&Ms, candy corn, super balls, raw kidney beans, or unpopped popcorn kernels.

How to Make a Smoke Screen with an Instant Cold Pack

WHAT YOU NEED

- Rubber gloves
- Safety goggles
- Scissors
- Instant cold pack (made with ammonium nitrate)
- Bucket
- Water (roughly 4 ounces)
- Newspaper
- Rubber bands (or pieces of string)
- Butane lighter or matches

WHAT TO DO

1. Wearing a pair of rubber gloves and safety goggles and using a pair of scissors, carefully cut open the instant cold pack. Inside you'll discover white granules of ammonium nitrate and a small plastic bag filled with water. *Do not ingest any ammonium nitrate and avoid contact with skin.*

2. Remove and discard the bag of water.
3. Pour the granules into the bucket.
4. Slowly add water and gently swirl the bucket until you have added just enough water to allow the ammonium nitrate granules to dissolve, creating a solution that is roughly 1 inch deep.
5. Fold a sheet of newspaper in half several times until it will fit into the bucket. Submerge the sheet of newspaper in the liquid to saturate it in the solution for a few minutes, remove it from the bucket, and gently reopen the sheet of newspaper. Lay it in the sun on a flat concrete surface (such as a driveway or sidewalk). To prevent breezes from blowing the newsprint away, place rocks or other weights on the four corners.

6. Repeat with additional sheets of newspaper until no more solution remains. Let the sheets of newspaper dry in the sun undisturbed for a few hours.

7. When the pages are completely dry, take a full sheet, fold it in half, roll it up into a tight tube, and secure it shut with a rubber band.

8. Using a butane lighter or matches, ignite one end of the newspaper tube, place it on the ground, and back away quickly. You can create additional tubes to light from the remaining sheets.

HOW IT WORKS

When ignited, the ammonium nitrate impregnated in the newspaper produces thick plumes of white smoke.

IN A FOG

- An instant cold pack consists of two bags. The first bag contains ammonium nitrate and an inner bag filled with water. Squeezing the package pops the inner bag, spilling the water into the larger bag, which dissolves the ammonium nitrate and triggers an endothermic reaction. That means the hydrated ammonium nitrate absorbs heat from the air inside the bag, making the bag cold.

- When heated, ammonium nitrate decomposes into nitrous oxide gas and water vapor.

- Ammonium nitrate, a common ingredient in fertilizer, can be mixed with certain hydrocarbons to make explosive bombs.

How to Camouflage Yourself with Shoe Polish

WHAT YOU NEED

- Makeup sponges
- Tin of brown, tan, and black shoe polish paste

WHAT TO DO

1. Using a makeup sponge or wedge, apply irregular, blotchy diagonal lines of shoe polish across your face, blending the color into your skin. Do not make a pattern.
2. Avoid applying shoe polish to your lips. Your lips should remain their natural color—and besides, unlike lipstick or lip balm, **shoe polish is far from edible**.
3. Around the eye area, apply light strokes, being careful **not to get shoe polish in your eyes**. If possible, wear sunglasses to cover your eyes to avoid applying shoe polish too closely around them.
4. Apply the makeup all the way down to your throat and around your neck, covering all exposed skin.
5. Don't forget to rub shoe polish on your ears (if they show) and on the space behind your ears. If you'd rather not rub shoe polish on your ears, wear your hair or a hat over your ears.
6. When you're finished applying shoe polish to your face and neck, rub shoe polish on your arms and the backs of your hands (not the palms).

HOW IT WORKS

Shoe polish contains bonding agents that cause it to adhere to your skin.

POLISH IT OFF

To remove shoe polish from your skin, apply a coat of vegetable shortening to your skin, let it sit for 15 minutes, and then rub the shortening into the skin with small circular motions. The vegetable shortening works like a solvent to dissolve the waxes and pigments in the shoe polish. Rinse clean with dishwashing detergent (which cuts through grease) and warm water. If the shoe polish remains on your face, wipe your face with baby wipes or a cotton ball dampened with isopropyl rubbing alcohol. The alcohol will dissolve more wax and pigment.

How to Assemble an Emergency Kit with an Altoids Tin

WHAT YOU NEED
- Empty Altoids tin

For an Automotive Kit
- Coins for parking meters

For a First Aid Kit
- Aspirin or other nonsteroidal anti-inflammatory drugs (NSAID)
- Adhesive bandages
- Alcohol swabs
- Small tube or packet of antibacterial ointment

For a Fix-It Kit
- Assorted screws and nuts
- Duct tape (wrapped around a short pencil or dowel)
- Miniature hammer
- Miniature screwdriver with detachable tips
- Swiss Army knife
- Zip ties

For a Key Kit
- Duplicate keys to the house, car, or strongbox

For a Sewing Kit
- 2 sewing needles
- Shirt buttons
- Safety pins
- Thread (various colors wrapped around a toothpick)

For a Survival Kit
- Small sheet of aluminum foil
- Batteries (AA)
- Bouillon cubes
- Candle (votive)
- Compass
- Duct tape
- Fishing kit: hook, fishing line, weight, and bobber
- Matches (waterproof) or butane lighter
- Miniature flashlight
- Disinfectant wipes
- Razor blade
- Signal mirror
- Small pen and paper
- Swiss Army knife
- Tea and coffee pouches
- Toothbrush
- Toothpaste
- Twist ties
- Whistle

WHAT TO DO

1. Fill a clean, empty Altoids tin, Tic Tac box, or plastic prescription pill bottle with any combination of the items listed above to make a compact emergency kit that best suits your anticipated needs.

2. To secure the lid of the Altoids tin shut, wrap it with a thick rubber band.

3. If making an emergency key kit, simply bury the canister (ideally a clean, waterproof, plastic prescription pill bottle) in an unforgettable spot in a garden plot in your yard.

4. If you're packing a survival kit, be sure to carry along a space blanket in your pocket, which can be used for both shelter and warmth.

HOW IT WORKS

An emergency kit stored in an Altoids tin, Tic Tac box, or plastic prescription pill bottle gives you the essential tools to survive. The conveniently sized case is easy to carry, store, and keep on hand at all times.

THINKING INSIDE THE BOX

- In an emergency, you can remove the lid from an empty Altoids tin, giving you a small container to boil water and a small pan to heat up food.
- You can also use an Altoids tin to hold a small deck of cards, dice, small poker chips, small pencils, and a small pad of paper for keeping score.
- A used Altoids tin can hold tea bags and instant coffee packets, sugar packets, ketchup and mustard packets, wrapped sticks of chewing gum, and other small food items.
- Engineers use Altoids tins for project box enclosures to hold do-it-yourself electronics devices, converting each tin into the home for an LED flashlight, a USB charger, or a stereo mixer.
- Tic Tac boxes can be used to store paper clips, thumb tacks, bobby pins and hair bands, buttons, ribbon, earrings, spices for camping, and beads.

How to Carve a Fake Gun from a Bar of Soap

WHAT YOU NEED

- Potato peeler (or food grater)
- Several bars of soap
- Clean, empty coffee can
- Water
- Saucepan
- Spoon
- Plastic or cardboard shoebox
- Cooking spray (for plastic shoebox)
- Waxed paper (for cardboard shoebox)
- Newspaper sheets
- Toothpick or pencil
- Plastic knife, fork, or spoon, or wooden Popsicle stick
- Black shoe polish paste

WHAT TO DO

1. Using the potato peeler, cut up the bars of soap into shreds.
2. Place the soap chips in a clean, empty coffee can, add a few ounces of water, and place the coffee can in a saucepan of simmering water.

3. Stir the soap with a spoon until the soap softens into a thick paste, similar to mashed potatoes. Add more water if necessary.

4. Spray the inside of a plastic shoebox with cooking spray or line a cardboard shoebox with waxed paper to create a mold for the melted soap.
5. Pour or spoon the melted soap into the mold. Pound the mold on the countertop a few times to remove air bubbles.

6. Let the soap harden and peel away the mold.
7. Cover your work area with sheets of newspaper.

8. Using a toothpick or pencil, draw an outline of the type of gun you intend to carve directly on one side of the bar of soap.

9. With the carving tool of your choice, gently whittle off small slivers of soap outside the outline, slicing away a small, slender piece with each cut. Otherwise, the soap may break off into chunks.

10. Carve the remaining soap into the shape of the gun.

11. Using the carving tool or the toothpick, add detail and texture to the soap gun to make the facsimile look authentic. Be sure to hollow the barrel of the fake gun.

12. When you're finished carving and detailing the soap gun, gently color the sculpted soap with black shoe polish paste. Gently rub the surface of the soap to create a smooth finish.

13. Let the soap dry and harden for 24 hours.

14. Add a second coat of black shoe polish and let the soap dry and harden for another 24 hours.

HOW IT WORKS

Melting soap and pouring it into a mold to reharden is called rebatching. Soap is soft and easily carved into various shapes with a carving tool. The black shoe polish paste, containing bonding agents, easily bonds to and colors the soap. From a distance, a bar of soap carved into the shape of gun, looks convincingly like a genuine firearm.

HAPPINESS IS A WARM SOAP GUN

- Contrary to popular belief, notorious gangster John Dillinger did not use a fake gun carved out of soap and painted black with shoe polish to escape from Lake County Jail in Crown Point, Indiana, on March 3, 1934. The fake gun was indeed painted black with shoe polish, but it was carved from wood.
- In the 1969 Woody Allen movie *Take the Money and Run*, Virgil Starkwell (Woody Allen) escapes from prison brandishing a gun carved out of soap, but when he gets caught in a rainstorm, the gun foams up, and the prisoner is returned to his cell.

How to Defend Yourself with a Ballpoint Pen

WHAT YOU NEED
- Ballpoint pen

WHAT TO DO
1. To defend yourself against an intruder or attacker intent on killing you, jab a ballpoint pen into the attacker's throat, eye, or chest to incapacitate the assailant long enough for you to escape.
2. Once you have reached safety, telephone 911 to report your act of self-defense and provide medical attention for the attacker.

HOW IT WORKS
Thrust with enough force, the sharp point of the pen doubles as a spear, turning the writing implement into a weapon.

MIGHTIER THAN THE SWORD
- Any thin, rigid object like a screwdriver, pencil, or toothpick becomes a weapon capable of producing a stab wound. Also, rolling pins, pots, and pans double as excellent clubs.

EVERY TRICK IN THE BOOK
Quill and Dagger
Scores of Hollywood movies and television shows depict a character stabbing someone with a pen or pencil. And the winners are:

- *Batman* (1989). The Joker (Jack Nicholson) kills a man by stabbing an ink quill pen into his throat.
- *The Bourne Identity* (2002). Jason Bourne (Matt Damon) disarms a knife-wielding assassin by stabbing him in the hand with a pen.
- *Casino* (1995). When a man in a bar insults Ace Rothstein (Robert DeNiro), Nicky Santoro (Joe Pesci) uses a pen to viciously stab the man in the throat.
- *24* (2009). In season 7, episode 23 ("6:00 AM–7:00 AM"), Kim Bauer (Elisha Cuthbert) stabs Sarah, a woman holding her hostage, with a pen.

How to Make a Dart Gun from a Ballpoint Pen

WHAT YOU NEED

- Ballpoint pen
- Scissors
- Thick rubber band
- Thin rubber band
- Sewing needle
- Scotch tape

WHAT TO DO

1. Dismantle the ballpoint pen entirely.
2. Using the scissors, cut the thick rubber band open to create a long rubber strip.

3. Place the middle of the rubber strip over the hole in one end of the pen barrel, hold the two ends of the rubber band against the length of the barrel, and slide the middle of the rubber band 1 inch away from the hole in the barrel.
4. Wrap the thin rubber band several times around the thick rubber band to secure it to the pen body.
5. Use the scissors to snip the excess from the thick rubber band.

6. Tape the sewing needle alongside the ballpoint end of the cartridge.
7. Insert the ink cartridge into the barrel of the pen gun with the hollow end of the ink cartridge facing the rubber band.
8. Aiming the barrel of the pen gun at your target, pinch the end of the rubber band and the end of the ink cartridge, and pull back like a slingshot.
9. To fire, simply let go of the rubber band and ink cartridge.

HOW IT WORKS

The spring action of the rubber band sends the ink cartridge flying through the barrel of the pen, which guides the ink cartridge on a trajectory toward your target. The tension of the rubber band sends the ink cartridge flying at a high speed for a significant distance.

WARNING

Never shoot the dart gun at any people or animals. The needle and ink cartridge can cause serious injury.

PEN PALS

- When making the pen gun, the two rubber bands can be replaced with the pinkie finger from a latex glove and a piece of duct tape.
- During discussion regarding gun legislation in Colorado's Senate Judiciary Committee in January 2013, State Senator Jessie Ulibarri noted that alternatives to guns for self-defense include ballpoint pens. Ulibarri pointed out that when a gunman stops to reload, if you haven't been shot, you can attack the assailant with a ballpoint pen.
- When a 22-year-old gunman shot Congresswoman Gabrielle Giffords and 18 others outside a Safeway supermarket in Tucson, Arizona, on January 8, 2011, unarmed shoppers took down the gunman with a lawn chair and ballpoint pens when he stopped to reload.

How to Avoid Detection from Thermal Imaging Cameras with a Space Blanket

WHAT YOU NEED
- Space blanket

WHAT TO DO
1. Crouch on the ground in a balled-up position.
2. Cover yourself with the space blanket with the shiny side facing you, tucking the edges of the tarp under your feet, legs, and arms—to contain all your body heat.
3. Remain under the metallic tarp until any drones or military trucks have left the area.

HOW IT WORKS
The space blanket doubles as a cloaking device by reflecting and containing your body heat, making your body heat less likely to be detected by thermal imaging cameras.

THE ULTIMATE SECURITY BLANKET
- Taliban insurgents in Afghanistan sometimes use space blankets to avoid detection from US thermal imaging cameras.
- Space blankets reflect and retain up to 80 percent of the human body's radiant heat.
- The Red Cross, military units, medical personnel, search-and-rescue groups, and various relief agencies use space blankets worldwide.

EVERY TRICK IN THE BOOK
Cool Uses for a Space Blanket

Invented in 1964 after a scientist at the National Research Corporation discovered that the metalized sheets of film used as external insulation on satellites and the Lunar Module could also keep people warm by reflecting heat back to the body, the space blanket has a wide array of alternative uses.

- **Car Heater.** If you get trapped in a car during a blizzard, cover the inside of the windshield with the space blanket with the shiny side facing inward to reflect your body heat back inside the car.
- **Car Sunscreen.** Improvise a reflective sunscreen for an automobile by covering the inside of the windshield with the space blanket with the shiny side facing out the window. The metallic surface reflects the heat of the sun out of the car.
- **Emergency Shelter.** In an emergency, use a space blanket to create an emergency shelter, such as a tent, tarp, or lean-to. The waterproof material repels rain or snow.
- **First Aid.** A space blanket can be used in an emergency situation for its intended purpose of keeping someone warm or preventing an individual from going into shock. To do so, wrap the blanket around the person, tucking in the sides under the body to retain heat and repel cold. To prevent additional heat loss, place a hat on the person's head.
- **Heat Reflector.** To combat cold temperatures, hang the blanket behind a fire or radiator so the shiny side reflects the heat back to you to help keep you warm.
- **Signal Mirror.** If you need to signal for help, use the reflective, shiny surface of the blanket as a signal mirror.
- **Snow Visor.** Cut a strip of the space blanket, and wrap it around your head as a pair of goggles. The see-through material doubles as sunglasses.
- **Sun Shade.** Hang the space blanket like a tarp with the shiny side facing upward to reflect sunlight and heat.
- **Tent Cooler.** To stay cool in a tent pitched in bright sunlight, cover the tent with the space blanket with the shiny side facing upward. The metallic surface reflects the heat away from the tent.
- **Windbreaker.** To protect yourself from cold winds, wrap a space blanket around your shoulders with the shiny side facing your body.

5

SURVIVAL TECHNIQUES

You find yourself shipwrecked on an uncharted island in the South Pacific, lost in the Amazon jungle, trapped in an arctic blizzard, stranded in the Sahara desert, confronted by a nuclear meltdown, or in the midst of a biological attack. Should you panic? Or calmly reach for the dental floss?

How to Protect Yourself from Nuclear Radiation with Iodine

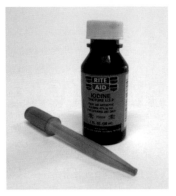

WHAT YOU NEED
- Potassium iodide tablets (or liquid)
- Water

WHAT TO DO

1. In the event of a nuclear reactor meltdown or a nuclear bomb blast, take potassium iodine in the following dosage (according to the Centers for Disease Control and Prevention):
   - Newborns up to 1 month of age: 16 mg (¼ of a 65 mg tablet or ¼ mL of solution).
   - Infants and children between 1 month and 3 years of age: 32 mg (½ of a 65 mg tablet or ½ mL of solution).
   - Children between 3 and 18 years of age (weighing less than 150 pounds): 65 mg (one 65 mg tablet or 1 mL of solution).
   - Adults, women who are breastfeeding, and children weighing 150 pounds or more: 130 mg (two 65 mg tablets or 2 mL of solution).
2. If you are exposed to radioactive iodine for more than 24 hours, take an additional dose of potassium iodide once every 24 hours for each day you are exposed. A single dose of potassium iodide protects the thyroid gland for 24 hours. Newborns and women who are pregnant or breastfeeding should not take more than one dose of potassium iodide.

HOW IT WORKS
The iodine flushes out and replaces any radioactive iodine in your system and prevents the thyroid gland from absorbing radioactive iodine-131. A thyroid gland full of natural iodine has no room to absorb iodine-131, protecting you against radiation-induced thyroid cancer.

RADIOACTIVITIES
- The thyroid, a small, butterfly-shaped gland in the neck, uses iodine to make a hormone that controls metabolism, regulating growth and development. The human body naturally absorbs iodine and stores it in the thyroid gland.

- A cloud of radioactive steam released by a faulty nuclear power plant contains an abundance of iodine-131—a radioactive form of iodine that causes thyroid cancer.
- When a failing nuclear power plant releases iodine-131 into the atmosphere, the thyroid—unable to differentiate radioactive iodine from nonradioactive iodine, absorbs and stores iodine-131 in the thyroid gland.
- If a faulty nuclear power plant releases radioactive steam into the atmosphere, people breathe in iodine-131. When radioactive particles settle onto plants, soil, and water, people eat fruits and vegetables tainted with iodine-131 and drink water containing the isotope. Cows that eat grass contaminated with iodine-131 produce milk that contains the radioactive element.
- The sooner you take potassium iodide after contamination, the quicker the thyroid will fill up with stable iodine.
- Taking a stronger dose of potassium iodide, or taking potassium iodide more often than recommended, does not provide any additional protection. Doing so can cause severe illness or even death.
- The side effects of taking potassium iodide may include stomach upset, allergic reactions, rashes, and inflammation of the salivary glands.
- Follow-up health studies conducted after the 1986 explosion and meltdown of the nuclear reactor at Chernobyl revealed a significant increase in thyroid cancer in the Chernobyl area, most notably among children who were under 10 years old at the time of the explosion. Children are most susceptible to the effects of iodine-131, possibly because their thyroid glands are still developing.
- Thyroid cancer is one of the least deadly forms of cancer. In the United States, approximately 5 percent of those who develop thyroid cancer die from the disease. Scientists have not yet determined mortality rates of radiation-induced thyroid cancer.

How to Defend Yourself from a Biological Attack with a Bra

WHAT YOU NEED
- Scissors
- Bra
- Binder clip

WHAT TO DO
1. Using a pair of scissors, cut the bra in half between the two cups.
2. Place one cup over your nose and mouth, with the support wire under your chin.
3. Wrap the back strap around your head (just below your ears), and attach the free end of the strap to the cup with a binder clip.

4. Stretch the spaghetti strap on top of your head.
5. Make sure the cup fits snugly. Place the palm of your hand over the cup and breathe deeply until the mask seals tightly to your face. Adjust the strap and binder clip if necessary.
6. Pinch the cup at the bridge of your nose to hold it in place.
7. Breathe normally through the fabric of the bra, holding the cup to your face if necessary.
8. Proceed to a safe location as quickly as possible.

HOW IT WORKS
The fabric in the bra cups filters out a variety of harmful airborne substances, depending, of course, on the make and manufacture of the undergarment.

YOUR CUP RUNNETH OVER
- For additional protection, line the inside of the cup with a coffee filter.
- In 2010, Ukrainian-born Chicago scientist Dr. Elena Bodnar launched a patented brassiere that can be worn as intended and then turned into a face mask to protect against lethal chemical attacks or biological hazards. To use the bra as a face mask to filter out harmful airborne substances, the wearer unsnaps the bra, which splits in half, converting the undergarment into two fully adjustable face masks.

How to Prevent Heatstroke with a Disposable Diaper

WHAT YOU NEED
- Disposable diaper
- Water

WHAT TO DO

1. If you can't rehydrate your body through osmosis (to prevent heatstroke) by taking a shower or jumping into a swimming pool, saturate a Pampers disposable diaper with water by filling a sink with water and submerging the diaper for 5 minutes. Or hold the two ends of the diaper like a hammock, fill the hammock with water from a faucet or water bottle, and rock the hammock until the superabsorbent polymer flakes inside the diaper become engorged and the diaper feels as heavy as a brick.

2. Wipe down your body with the saturated diaper to give yourself a refreshing sponge bath and rehydrate your skin.

3. Wear the waterlogged diaper on your head or around the back of your neck to replenish your body with moisture and cool your body temperature.

HOW IT WORKS

Pampers diapers are filled with superabsorbent polymer flakes that absorb up to 300 times their weight in water. Because the polymer requires more time than paper to absorb liquid, scientists added an absorbent paper liner before the core to hold the liquid until the polymer fully absorbs it. Under the first thin layer of absorbent padding is a layer of polyfilm, a thin, woven polyresin whose fibers channel the liquid toward the absorbent core. The pores in the polyfilm are big enough to let air flow in, allowing the diaper to breathe, but small enough to keep liquid from flowing out, preventing the diaper from leaking. Holding the wet diaper against your body allows your skin cells to absorb the water through osmosis. The coolness also lowers your body temperature.

COMING UP FROM BEHIND

During the Gulf War in 1990, American soldiers saturated disposable diapers (sent from home) with water to give themselves sponge baths, treat heat exhaustion, and avoid dehydration in the blistering hot deserts of Saudi Arabia.

How to Make Warm Clothes with a Bath Mat and Bubble Wrap

WHAT YOU NEED

- Bath mat
- Scissors
- Belt (or 36-inch length of rope)
- Bubble Wrap (or newspaper)
- Rubber bands

WHAT TO DO

1. Fold a carpeted bath mat in half.
2. Using the scissors, carefully cut a 10-inch crescent in the middle of the fold to create a hole for your head.
3. Wear the bath mat over your head as a poncho.
4. Hold the bath mat in place with a belt (or by tying a rope) around your waist.
5. Using the scissors, cut several strips of Bubble Wrap 3 inches wide and 30 inches long. At one end of each of the 30-inch lengths, cut two 2-inch vertical slots for belt loops.
6. Insert the Bubble Wrap strips into the legs of your long pants with the "slots" extending out over the waist. Fold back the ends and thread your belt (or a rope) through the slots to hold up the strips.
7. If you don't have any Bubble Wrap, shove crumpled-up sheets of newspaper down the legs of your pants.
8. Tuck your pant legs into your socks, or wrap a rubber band around the bottom of each pant leg, to retain heat and prevent the newspaper from falling out of the pant legs.

HOW IT WORKS

Layers of clothing, such as the bath mat poncho, create layers of air, which are warmed by your body heat. Padding the space between your body and your clothes with Bubble Wrap or crumpled newspaper provides insulation, raising the temperature of the air layer.

DRESS FOR EXCESS

- If you don't have access to newspaper, you can use dry leaves as insulation. Check the leaves to make sure you're not putting any bugs down your pants.
- Ideally, stuff the insulation between layers of clothing, such as between long underwear and trousers or between a shirt and a sweater. This helps to minimize the itch factor.
- You can also insulate yourself by wearing large plastic trash bags over your body as a waterproof windbreaker. The plastic bags trap your body heat.
- In the 1989 movie *Parenthood*, Gil Buckman (Steve Martin) improvises a cowboy costume by fashioning chaps from a carpeted bath mat.

How to Make a Compass with a Cork and Needle

WHAT YOU NEED

- Knife
- Cork (or the plastic cap from a soda or water bottle, or the bottom of a Styrofoam cup)
- Needle (or straightened paper clip)
- Refrigerator magnet (or the magnet from an electric can opener, cabinet door, or purse clasp)
- Saucer, bowl, or saucepan
- Water
- Dishwashing liquid

WHAT TO DO

1. Using the knife, carefully slice a circle-shaped piece (no more than ¼ inch thick) from the larger end of the cork.
2. Holding the flat end of the needle, stroke the sharpened half of the needle against one pole of the magnet sixty times.
3. Carefully holding the sharp end of the needle (to avoid pricking yourself), stroke the other half of the needle against the opposite pole of the magnet 60 times.
4. Insert the needle through the sides of the cork slice (or lay the needle on top of the cork).
5. Fill the saucer, bowl, or saucepan with 1 inch of water and add a drop of dishwashing liquid to the water in the center of the bowl.
6. Place the cork in the center of the saucer of water.
7. Observe as the floating cork turns until the needle points in a north-south direction.

HOW IT WORKS

The Earth's magnetosphere, the magnetic field around the planet, has two magnetic poles, located near the North and South Poles. Rubbing a sewing needle with a magnet magnetizes the needle, and the freely suspended magnet, floating on a cork in a dish of still water, points to the Earth's magnetic north pole. A drop of dishwashing liquid in the water dispels the surface tension of the water, causing the cork to float freely in the center of the saucer.

DETERMINE YOUR DIRECTION WITH A PENCIL

With just a pencil, pen, drinking straw, or stick of any kind, you can use the sun and time-lapse plotting to ascertain directions. Stick a pencil in the ground. Place a small stone or a coin on the top end of the pencil's shadow. Wait approximately 15 minutes until the top end of the pencil moves a couple of inches. Place another stone or coin on the top end of the shadow tip's new position. Draw a straight line through the two stones or coins. The line indicates an approximate east-west direction. Since the sun rises in the east and sets in the west, the first shadow tip will be west of the second shadow tip. A line drawn perpendicular to the east-west line will point approximately north-south. Whether the ground slopes or the stick leans to one side makes no difference.

GOT THE TIME?

As the sun nears the horizon before sunset, you can guesstimate how much time remains before sundown by stretching your arm straight out in front of you, palm forward. Keep your fingers together and position your hand horizontally between the horizon and the sun. If there's still room between them, place your other hand on top of the first. The width of each finger between the horizon and bottom of the sun measures approximately 15 minutes before sunset. In other words, if the sun sits the width of three fingers above the horizon, you have roughly 45 minutes before sunset (depending upon your latitude on Earth and the time of year).

How to Make an Emergency Lantern with Baby Oil and a Tampon

WHAT YOU NEED
- Clean, empty coffee can (or glass jar)
- Dirt or sand
- Tampon
- Baby oil, vegetable oil, or fat from cooked bacon or any other meat
- Butane lighter or matches

WHAT TO DO

1. Fill a clean, empty coffee can with tightly packed dirt or sand to within an inch of the rim.
2. Remove a tampon from its wrapper, discard the cardboard or plastic applicator, and push the tampon into the dirt or sand with the string sticking up from the dirt.
3. Pour baby oil, vegetable oil, or bacon or meat fat into the can.
4. Light the tampon string.

HOW IT WORKS

The tampon wicks up the oil or grease in this hobo lantern, burning long and bright.

SEE THE LIGHT
- If you can't locate any dry dirt or sand due to rainy weather, simply fill the can or glass jar with the oil or grease, push the tampon into the oil with the string visible above the surface, and light the end of the string.
- To prevent the wind from blowing out this lantern or a candle, use a knife or pair of scissors to cut off the bottom of a clean, empty 2-liter soda bottle. Place the bottomless, uncapped bottle over the lantern or candle flame, without letting the flame melt the plastic. The bottle functions as a transparent windscreen, preventing the wind from blowing

out the flame, without cutting off the oxygen supply that keeps the flame burning.

- To turn a coffee can into a portable lantern, remove the bottom from the coffee can and turn the coffee can on its side. Attach a handle to the "top" by punching two holes (one near the top rim and another near the bottom rim), make a handle from a wire coat hanger and loop it through the holes. Using a sharp knife, cut a 2-inch-tall X in the center of the bottom. Push a candle through the X so the wick sits in the center of the can. Light the candle and carry or hang the lantern by the handle. The shiny metal inside the coffee can reflects the flame, creating a surprisingly bright light. The can also shields the flame from wind. When the candle burns low, simply push the candle farther up into the can.

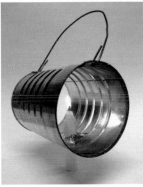

- To make a decorative coffee can lantern, fill a clean, empty coffee can with water and place it in the freezer until the water turns to ice. Remove the can from the freezer and, using hammer and a nail, punch holes in the can in whatever design you desire. The ice inside the can prevents the can from collapsing when you hit it with the hammer and nail. When you're finished punching holes in the can, let the ice melt. Then place a votive candle in the bottom of the can, light it, and enjoy the design emanating from the lit holes.

How to Collect Rainwater with a Trash Bag

WHAT YOU NEED

- Scissors or knife
- Plastic trash bag
- Four sticks
- Rope, string, or dental floss
- Small stone
- Bucket or other container

WHAT TO DO

1. Using the scissors or knife, slice open the trash bag along one side and the bottom to make one large plastic sheet. If you don't have a trash bag, use whatever material you have, such as a plastic shower curtain, a poncho, a space blanket, or a tarp.
2. Spread the sheet open on the ground.
3. Insert four sticks into the ground at the corners of the plastic sheet.
4. Using rope, cord, or dental floss, secure each corner of the plastic sheet to its corresponding stick, raising the plastic sheet off the ground but allowing one end of the plastic sheet to rise higher than the other.
5. Place a small stone in the center of the plastic sheet to create a gutter, so that all collected rainwater will flow toward the center of the plastic sheet and then flow toward the middle of the two lower sticks.
6. Place a bucket or container under the lower center of the plastic sheet to collect the rainwater.
7. Filter and purify the water before drinking.

HOW IT WORKS

The suspended waterproof sheet catches the rainwater, and the stone weight diverts the flow of water like a gutter, allowing you to capture more fresh water during a light rainfall and many gallons of fresh water in just a few minutes during a heavy rainfall.

ALL WET

- You can also capture fresh water during a rainstorm by setting out open containers, such as buckets, soda bottles with the tops cut off, cans, bowls, and pots. Or use long pieces of curved bark as gutters to direct the flow of water while the rain falls.
- If you're unable to suspend a plastic sheet above the ground, find four short logs and arrange them to make a square. Position rocks against the logs to prevent them from rolling, if necessary. Then drape the plastic sheet over the logs, forming a catch basin. Or dig a hole roughly 4 feet in diameter and 1 foot deep, and line it with the plastic sheet.
- After a rainstorm, use a spoon, a small cup, or a piece of plastic tubing to collect water from depressions in rocks, logs, and other places where puddles of water have accumulated.
- To collect dew, wipe a bandana (or a cotton T-shirt) over dew-covered leaves and grass. When the bandana is soaking wet, squeeze out the collected dew into a container. To make collecting dew from grass easier, tie a bandana around each one of your ankles and walk through the grass.
- To melt snow into water, fill a black trash bag with snow and lay the bag in direct sunlight. The black bag absorbs the heat from the sun, melting the snow.
- To make a water scoop, cut off the top of a clean, used waxed cardboard milk carton.
- Filter debris from water by pouring the water through a plastic funnel lined with a coffee filter.
- To purify water at sea level, simply bring it to a rolling boil for 1 full minute. For each 1,000-foot rise in elevation, add 1 minute of boiling time.
- To purify water by adding liquid chlorine bleach, add five drops of household bleach (containing 5.25 to 8.25 percent chlorine) for each quart of water, mix thoroughly, and let the treated water stand for at least 60 minutes before drinking. For 1 gallon of water, add ¼ teaspoon of bleach.
- To remove musty odors from a canteen or water, put 3 teaspoons of baking soda in the container, fill the rest of the container with water, and shake vigorously. Let it sit for 1 hour and then rinse clean.

How to Desalinate Water with Plastic Wrap

WHAT YOU NEED

- Clean, empty coffee can
- Bucket
- Dish towel, clean rags, or a clean T-shirt
- Seawater
- Plastic wrap
- Small stone or a few coins

WHAT TO DO

1. Stand the coffee can in the center of the bucket.
2. Soak the dish towel, rags, or T-shirt with seawater and place it on the floor of the bucket, wrapped around the coffee can—without getting any saltwater inside the can.
3. Stretch a sheet of plastic wrap over the mouth of the bucket, making it taut and airtight around the rim of the bucket.
4. Place a small stone or a few coins in the center of the sheet of plastic wrap so that the sheet dips like a cone, with its vertex pointing directly over the center of the coffee can.
5. Set the bucket in direct sunlight for several hours.

HOW IT WORKS

The heat from the sun causes the seawater to evaporate, leaving the salt particles in the cloth at the bottom of the bucket. The evaporated water condenses on the underside of the plastic wrap and then that fresh water drips into the can.

SALT OF THE EARTH

- If you're stranded at sea, you can also collect rainwater by setting up as many open containers as possible to collect the water. Be sure to use heavy objects to steady the containers and prevent the rocking of the boat from toppling over the containers.
- More than 97.5 percent of the water on Earth contains salt.
- Humans can safely drink water that contains less that 0.5 percent salt. Seawater contains approximately 3.5 percent salt.
- A person who drinks only seawater will die of thirst. The kidneys cannot filter out all of the salt, and the body will dehydrate.
- Saltwater can be desalinated through distillation, reverse osmosis, electrodialysis, and freezing.

How to Build a Water Purification Still with a Trash Bag

WHAT YOU NEED

- Shovel
- Clean, empty coffee can (or bucket)
- Plastic tubing
- Scissors or knife
- Plastic trash bag
- Stones, logs, or dirt
- Small stone or a few coins

WHAT TO DO

1. Dig a hole 3 feet in diameter and 2 feet deep.
2. In the center of the hole, dig a small hole to hold the coffee can in position. Place the coffee can in the small hole inside the large hole.

3. Place one end of the plastic tube in the coffee can and run the other end of the tube out of the hole, beyond the edge.
4. Using the scissors or knife, slice open the trash bag along one side and the bottom to make one large plastic sheet. If you don't have a trash bag, use whatever material you have, such as a plastic shower curtain, poncho, space blanket, or tarp.
5. Drape the plastic sheet over the large hole, making sure not to cover up the free end of the tube. Anchor the plastic sheet in place with stones, logs, or dirt. Make sure the plastic sheet covers the entire hole without any gaps around the edge that could let water vapor escape from the hole.
6. Place a small stone or several coins in the center of the plastic sheet so that the sheet dips like a cone with its vertex pointing directly over the center of the coffee can.
7. Wait a few hours and then suck on the free end of the tube to pull the purified water from the coffee can.

HOW IT WORKS

The heat from the sun raises the temperature of the air and soil in the hole under the plastic sheet, turning any moisture in the ground into vapor, which rises and condenses as purified water on the underside of the plastic wrap. The droplets of water run down the underside of the plastic and drip into the can.

PURE AND SIMPLE

- Soils retain water, which plants and other organisms use to flourish. Gravity drains some of this water from the soil, carrying it to streams, rivers, and other waterways.
- Different particles of soil retain different amounts of water.
- Data from the Mars rover *Curiosity*, published in the journal *Science* in October 2013, suggests that the soil from the Martian surface contains approximately 2 percent water by weight. In other words, if you ever find yourself stranded on Mars without any water, you might be able to build a water purification still to tap the Martian soil for water.

How to Make a Transpiration Still with a Trash Bag

WHAT YOU NEED

- Small stones
- Large, clear plastic trash bag
- String, twine, or cord

WHAT TO DO

1. Locate a large deciduous tree or bush—making certain that the plant is not poisonous. The larger the tree or bush is, the larger the root system is (gathering more water).
2. Select the side of the tree or bush that will receive the most sunlight for the rest of the day.
3. Drop a small stone inside a large, clear plastic trash bag.
4. Pull together a bunch of leafy branches of the tree or bush and place the trash bag over them so that you've fit as many leafy branches as possible inside the bag.
5. Make sure the small stone inside the plastic bag sits in the bottom corner of the bag, away from the leafy vegetation, creating a lone pocket of air.
6. Seal the mouth of the plastic trash bag tightly around the tree limb, making sure no outside air can get into the bag. Use the string, twine, or cord to tie off the neck of the bag tightly around the tree limb.
7. Pull down the corner of the bag containing the stone, creating a pocket where the water will collect. If necessary, tie another piece of string, twine, or cord around the stone (and the corner of the plastic bag), and stake it in the ground or tie it to the trunk of the tree or bush, or another low-lying plant.
8. Let this sit for several hours. Depending on the intensity of the sun and clouds, a large plastic bag will yield an average of 1 to 2 cups of water in a day.
9. To be safe, filter and purify the water before drinking.

HOW IT WORKS

The sun shines through the clear plastic bag, heating up the air inside the bag and causing the plant leaves to transpire, giving off water vapor through the stomata. The purified water condenses on the inside walls of the plastic bag and then drips down to the corner weighted down by the stone. The leaves of the tree will provide water for two to three days.

BARKING UP THE RIGHT TREE

- The more transpiration bags you set up, the more water you'll collect.
- Filter out debris and insects from the water through a bandana or coffee filter.
- Rather than removing the bag to retrieve the water, use duct tape to attach a short plastic tube or drinking straw to the corner to drain collected water from the bag. Plug the end of the tube or straw by crimping it with a binder clip or inserting a small stopper, perhaps whittled from a stick.

How to Transport Water with a Cardboard Box

WHAT YOU NEED

- Empty cardboard box
- Plastic trash bag

WHAT TO DO

1. Remove the top of the cardboard box, or fold the top cardboard flaps inside the box.
2. Place the open cardboard box upside down inside the plastic trash bag.
3. Pull the plastic cord tightly to seal the mouth of the trash bag shut. Tie the cord securely.
4. Turn the sealed trash bag upside down and set it on the ground so the tied cord rests under the box and the cardboard box within the bag sits upright.
5. Push the plastic covering the open side into the box so that the trash bag is lining the inside.
6. Fill the plastic-lined box with water to within 2 inches of the top.
7. Carry the plastic-wrapped box of water to wherever you need.

HOW IT WORKS

Wrapping a cardboard box inside a plastic trash bag converts a porous and absorbent cardboard box into a waterproof bucket.

THAT DOESN'T HOLD WATER

- Fill a condom with water, like a water balloon, to transport or store water in this expandable container.
- Let cloudy water settle before filtering it or treating it with chemicals. Doing so allows debris and sediment to sink to the bottom.
- After treating water with chemicals, wait at least 30 minutes to give the chemicals ample time to kill any germs in the water.
- Never drink from a stagnant pool of water near dead fish or other animals. Something in the water may have poisoned them—and may poison you as well.
- Collect water from a stream, river, pond, or lake that supports healthy, green plant life.
- Never consider running or cascading water safe to drink until you filter and purify it. Even fresh mountain stream water contains germs that can make you severely ill.

How to Filter Water with a Soda Bottle

WHAT YOU NEED
- Knife or scissors
- Clean, empty 1- or 2-liter soda bottle
- Dental floss, cord, or wire
- Coffee filter (or small piece of paper towel)
- Gravel
- Sand

WHAT TO DO
1. Using a knife or scissors, carefully cut off the bottom of the soda bottle.
2. Cut two holes at opposite sides of the bottle approximately 1 inch from the edge that you cut from the bottom.
3. Tie a piece of dental floss, cord, or wire through the two holes, creating a handle from which you can hang the upside-down bottle from a tree branch.
4. Place a coffee filter inside the bottle to cover the hole in the bottleneck.
5. Add a 2-inch layer of gravel in the bottle, followed by a 2-inch layer of sand.
6. Repeat step 4, and add a final 2-inch layer of gravel.
7. Hang the bottle from a tree branch.
8. Place a container under the mouth of the bottle as a catch basin.
9. Collect water from a river, lake, puddle, or any other source, and slowly pour it into the top of the filter, letting it trickle down through the layers of gravel and sand and into the catch basin.
10. Boil the filtered water.

HOW IT WORKS
The alternating layers of gravel and sand filter debris from the water.

TEST THE WATERS
- You can also filter water through the leg cut from a pair of panty hose. Remove the bottom from a clean, empty soup can, place the panty hose leg inside the can, fold the rim of the panty hose leg over the top of the

can, and hold it in place with a rubber band, a zip tie, or someone else's hands. Hold the device over a container and pour the water through the panty hose leg to filter out dirt particles or vegetation.

- You can also filter out debris from water through a bandana, coffee filter, or T-shirt.
- A tampon can serve as a water-filtration system. Pull apart the tampon to expose all the fibers; cut off the bottom of a clean, empty 2-liter bottle to create a funnel; and insert the tampon into the neck of the bottle.

EVERY TRICK IN THE BOOK

Cheap Cookware

- **Double Boiler.** To fashion a double boiler for melting paraffin wax, bend a wire clothes hanger so it will support a clean, empty 1-pound coffee can inside a clean, empty 2-pound coffee can. Fill the larger can halfway with water, place the paraffin inside the smaller can, place both cans over heat, and bring the water to a rolling boil until the wax melts.
- **Frying Pan.** To make a poor man's frying pan, remove the label from a clean, empty tuna fish can, and wrap a wire  clothes hanger around the can to fashion a handle. Use the miniature frying pan to melt butter or heat up single servings of meat loaf, potatoes, or soup.
- **Kettle.** Turn a coffee can into a kettle by punching two holes on opposite sides of the can, just under the top rim. Bend a length of wire hanger into the crescent shape of a handle, and loop the ends through the holes in the can.
- **Toaster.** To convert a coffee can into a toaster, use a hammer and nail to punch eight evenly spaced holes around the sides of the can, just under the top rim. Straighten a wire clothes hanger, cut off four 6-inch lengths, and insert the strips of wire through the holes to create a tic-tac-toe board pattern. Set the toaster over a bed of hot coals and place a slice of bread on the grill.

How to Build a Stove with a Tuna Fish Can

WHAT YOU NEED

- Clean, empty coffee can
- Tin snips
- Can opener (or hammer and nail)
- Scissors
- Corrugated cardboard
- Clean, empty tuna fish can and detached lid
- Candle or block of paraffin wax
- Pot
- Clean, empty soup can
- Tongs or a heavy weight
- Birthday candle (optional)
- Matches or butane lighter

WHAT TO DO

1. Turn the coffee can upside down, and using the tin snips, cut a 2-inch-by-2½-inch door along the bottom of the can, leaving the top seam of the door uncut as the hinge of the door.
2. Bend the metal flap up to open the door.
3. Still holding the can upside down, use a can opener to punch several holes around the top rim to allow smoke to escape. (Or use a hammer and nail to punch holes in the top of the can.)

4. Using the scissors, cut the corrugated cardboard into long strips the same width as the height of the tuna fish can. Be sure to cut the strips so that the interior fluting runs across the width of the strips and the holes in the fluting show at the sides.
5. Roll the strips into a tight coil that fits snugly inside the tuna fish can.
6. Melt the candle or paraffin wax by filling a pot halfway with water, setting a clean, empty soup can in the water, and placing the wax in the can. Holding the can in place with a pair of tongs or a heavy weight, bring the water to a rolling boil.

7. Carefully pour the melted wax into the tuna fish can to fill the fluted holes in the cardboard, saturate the cardboard, and fill the can to the brim.
8. Place a wick made from a small piece of leftover cardboard or a birthday candle in the center of the cardboard coil.
9. Let the wax cool and harden. The tuna fish can is now a buddy burner.

10. Set the buddy burner on a solid, nonflammable surface, such as concrete, bricks, large rocks, or dirt ground.
11. With a butane lighter or match, light the wick. The flame will engulf the top of the entire can.
12. Place the prepared coffee can (also known as a hobo stove) over the buddy burner.
13. By adjusting the door on the coffee can (which serves as a damper), you can control the intensity of the fire and maintain the desired temperature.
14. Use a small frying pan to cook on top of the stove, or fry bacon and eggs directly on top of the coffee can.
15. When you finish cooking, use the detached lid of the tuna fish can to extinguish the flame.

HOW IT WORKS
The hobo stove retains heat and distributes it evenly across the metal cooking surface. The fire, contained within the coffee can, generates and transfers an enormous amount to the cooking surface.

CHIEF COOK AND BOTTLE WASHER
- If you don't have a buddy burner, you can use pencils, thick sticks, twigs, woodchips, or charcoal briquettes for fuel.
- The origin of the hobo stove coincided with the invention of the No. 10 tin can. During the Depression, hobos and vagabonds relied upon the No. 10 tin can as a vital tool of survival. They resourcefully used the tin can as a stove, water bucket, serving dish, suitcase, and storage container.

How to Construct an Oven with Aluminum Foil and Clothes Hangers

WHAT YOU NEED

- 8 lengths of wire coat hanger, 14 inches each
- Ruler
- Standard photocopy paper cardboard box with slip-on cardboard lid
- Heavy-duty aluminum foil
- Stapler (optional)
- Pliers
- Hot coals from a fire (or 9 hot charcoal briquettes)
- Cake or pie pan
- Matches or butane lighter
- Cooking thermometer
- Timer

WHAT TO DO

1. Using the end of one of the lengths of wire, puncture eight holes in each 18-inch side of the box, spacing the holes 2 inches apart and 3 inches from the top of the box. (These holes will later support the grill wires.)

2. Line the inside of the cardboard box and lid with heavy-duty aluminum foil, with the shiny side facing out. Make sure you cover all the cardboard with aluminum foil. Otherwise, the cardboard box might combust. (If desired, you can fasten the foil to the inside of the box with staples.)

3. Insert each wire through the two opposite prepunched holes to form the grill. Using pliers, bend over the ends of each wire to hold them in place.

4. Carefully put hot coals from a wood fire in the cake or pie pan.

5. Carefully slide the cake or pie pan between the wires of the grill and set it in the center of the floor of the box.
6. Raise the pan off the floor of the box by placing the pan on top of a few rolled-up balls of aluminum foil.
7. Place whatever you wish to bake on the grill and close the lid.
8. To measure the temperature inside the oven, insert a cooking thermometer through the lid of the box.
9. Set a timer for the baking time required. If the baking time requires more than 45 minutes, add more hot coals or replace the charcoal at the 45-minute mark.

HOW IT WORKS

The aluminum foil reflects the heat of the hot coals, turning the box into a convection oven.

HOME ON THE RANGE

- Each hot charcoal briquette raises the temperature inside the box approximately 40°F. Nine briquettes supply 360°F inside the oven.
- If you're using charcoal briquettes to heat the oven, you can adjust the temperature inside the oven by simply calibrating the number of charcoal briquettes necessary. For instance, if a recipe calls for 280°F, divide 280°F by 40°F per briquette to determine that seven briquettes will achieve the desired temperature.
- When using the oven, monitor the cardboard box in case you neglected to properly cover the inside with aluminum foil and the box begins to smolder or catches fire.

How to Build a Life Raft with Soda Bottles

WHAT YOU NEED

- Door
- 50 clean, empty 2-liter soda bottles with caps
- Duct tape
- Tennis racket
- Ping Pong paddle
- Broomstick
- Folding chair or ice chest (optional)

WHAT TO DO

1. Unscrew a hollow core door from the jamb inside your house. Remove the hinges and the doorknob.
2. Line up the empty soda bottles, caps on, and duct tape them to one side of the door. Alternatively, you can place smaller plastic jugs and bottles inside a plastic trash bag, pull the cords tightly, and secure the trash bag to the door.

3. Use duct tape to attach a Ping Pong paddle to a broomstick to create an oar. Or use a tennis racket inside its case.

4. For seating, add a folding chair or an ice chest to the other side of the door.

HOW IT WORKS

The empty soda bottles double as buoyancy cells. Each 2-liter bottle displaces roughly 4 pounds of water. Divide your weight by 4 pounds to calculate how many bottles you'll need for your raft to keep you afloat. For instance, a man weighing 180 pounds will need 45 bottles. However, that's merely enough bottles to keep the boat afloat without any wiggle room. For safety, add 20 percent to your weight (in this case 36 pounds, for a total of 216 pounds, requiring 54 bottles) to guarantee that the raft floats with you aboard.

ROW YOUR BOAT

If your home is filling with water and you need a life raft to escape, you can use any of these items as an impromptu life raft:

- Mattress
- Dining room table (turned upside down)
- Ice chest
- Plastic swimming pool
- Spare tire
- Large plastic tub

How to Kindle a Fire with Chocolate and a Soda Can

WHAT YOU NEED
- Clean, empty aluminum soda can
- Chocolate bar
- Paper towel or rag
- Tinder (or toilet paper)
- Kindling

WHAT TO DO
1. Note that the bottom of the soda can looks unfinished and unpolished, with fine lines in the aluminum.
2. Rub the chocolate all over the bottom of the soda can.
3. Using a paper towel or rag, wipe off the chocolate, polishing the bottom of the can to a glimmering shine. (**Do not eat the chocolate** after rubbing it against the can. The chocolate removes the oxide layer on the surface of the aluminum, exposing the bare metal, which can be toxic.)
4. Repeat the process several times until the bottom of the can shines with a mirror finish. (If you hold an object close to the bottom of the can, you should see a clear image distorted by the curvature of the can.)
5. Find a direct ray of sunlight and angle the can to make sure its bottom reflects the sun's rays. If not, continue polishing.
6. Place tinder in an appropriate spot, and hold the can 1 or 2 inches away from the center of the tinder, using the bottom of the can to reflect the concentrated beam of sunlight onto the tinder. The focal point of the concave mirror created by the bottom of the can should converge the concentrated light from the sun approximately 1 inch away from the can.
7. Hold the can in position for a few seconds until the tinder begins to smoke and smolder. Gently blow air at the tinder to start a flame, and slowly add kindling to the fire.

HOW IT WORKS
The dull finish on the bottom of a soda can is not shiny enough to reflect and concentrate the sun's rays to ignite tinder. In fact, the fine lines on

the unpolished aluminum would scatter the sun's rays, rather than focus them together into a single bright point. The chocolate, however, polishes up the bottom of the can, allowing it to reflect and concentrate the sun's light and energy.

GOING DOWN IN FLAMES

- If you don't have any chocolate, you can also polish the bottom of the soda can with toothpaste, fine steel wool, or any powdered cleanser.
- You can also start a fire with a flashlight reflector. Remove the reflector from the flashlight, place tinder (or toilet paper) in the hole in the center of the reflector where the bulb normally goes, and aim the reflector at the sun to converge the rays of sunlight on the end of the tinder until it smolders. A cigarette pushed up from the back of the hole also makes effective tinder.

FIRE AWAY

- To build a fire, find a spot on dry land protected from wind and precipitation. If necessary, dig a fire pit. If the ground is wet, build a dry platform with some logs.
- Before building a fire, gather tinder, kindling, and large pieces of wood. For tinder, bundle dry grasses into the shape of a bird's nest. For kindling, collect small, dry twigs and sticks the size of a wood pencil, or find several 1-inch-thick sticks and use a knife to cut slices that remain attached to the stick and curl away from it, creating what are called fuzz sticks. For large pieces of wood, gather dry branches the size of your forearm.
- Place the tinder bundle on the ground, and build a tepee of kindling over it, leaving space between the sticks for the fire to breathe. Keep the large pieces of wood nearby.
- To light the fire, kneel by the tinder and kindling. Using your body to shield against the wind, use a match or butane lighter to ignite the tinder. Add more kindling to the fire, generating a strong blaze, and once the fire takes hold, gradually add larger pieces of wood.
- To roll your own newspaper logs using a broom, unscrew the broomstick from the bristles, fold two or three sheets of newsprint in half, and wrap them around the broomstick as tightly as possible. When you roll the newsprint 2 inches thick, tie the roll with string, dental floss, wire, or twist ties. Remove the broomstick. Use the thin log as a fire starter, or make a heftier log by wrapping more newspaper around it until the roll is 5 or 6 inches thick and secure with more string, floss, or wire.

How to Start a Fire with Petroleum Jelly and Cotton Balls

WHAT YOU NEED
- Cotton balls
- Petroleum jelly
- Matches or butane lighter

WHAT TO DO
1. Coat the cotton balls with petroleum jelly, working the jelly into the cotton balls without saturating them.
2. Tear off a small piece of the jellied cotton ball (or use the entire cotton ball) and place it under a stack of dry or damp twigs.
3. Ignite the cotton with a match or butane lighter.

HOW IT WORKS
These highly flammable cotton balls ignite quickly and easily with a spark because they have a low flash point. They burn for several minutes, drying damp kindling and igniting a campfire quickly and efficiently.

STARTING FROM SCRATCH
- To travel with these prepared cotton balls, store them in an airtight container, such as a clean, empty plastic prescription pill bottle.
- Alcohol pads from a first aid kit can be used as tinder to start a fire or as a short-term candle. Cut a small X in the center of the package, and pull some of the alcohol pad up through the X to create a wick.
- Disinfectant hand wipes or baby wipes can also be used as tinder to start a fire.
- If you're having difficulty lighting a fire, squirt some liquid hand sanitizer on the tinder and ignite it. The flammable ethyl alcohol in the sanitizer burns hot.
- An empty butane lighter can still be used as a flint sparker. Strike the lighter, and the spark will ignite well-prepared tinder, such as a cotton ball coated with petroleum jelly.
- To create convenient, inexpensive kindling, take the leftover cardboard tubes from rolls of paper towels or toilet paper and stuff them with wastepaper.

- To make easy-to-use emergency kindling, cut a clean, empty, waxed cardboard milk or juice carton into slivers. Wrap the slivers in a ziplock storage bag and keep them handy.

- Make highly effective fire starters by cutting 3-inch-long strips of corrugated cardboard 1 inch wide so that the interior fluting runs across the width of the strips and the holes in the fluting show at the sides. Insert wooden matches in every other hole created by the fluting, dip the strips in melted paraffin wax, and let dry.

MEET YOUR MATCH

- To waterproof matches, burn a candle until a pool of wax forms around the wick. Blow out the flame and individually dip the heads of your matches into the wet wax to give them a light coating of wax. Remove the match from the pool of hot wax and let the wax dry on the match head.

- Another way to waterproof matches is to coat the heads with clear nail polish. Simply dip the head of the match into the polish, lay the match on a counter with the head jutting off the edge, and let it dry.

- You can also make matches waterproof by soaking them in turpentine for 5 minutes. Afterward, set the matches on newspaper to dry. Soaking matches in turpentine draws out the water in the head and matchstick stem. Matches treated this way remain waterproof for several months.

- To keep matches dry, store them in waterproof plastic prescription pill bottles.

How to Pick Fruit from a Tree with a Bleach Jug

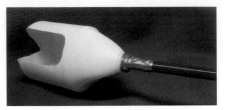

WHAT YOU NEED

- Knife or scissors
- Clean, empty bleach jug
- Broomstick
- Duct tape
- Bubble Wrap (or cloth)

WHAT TO DO

1. Use a knife or pair of scissors to carefully cut out a sector (resembling a slice of pizza from a pizza cut into eight slices) from the bottom of the bleach jug. Discard the plastic slice.

2. From the two ends of the sector at the circumference of the bottle bottom, cut a U shape into the side of the bleach bottle, roughly 4 inches in height.

3. Insert one end of the broomstick into the mouth of the jug. Wrap duct tape around the broomstick and the neck of the jug to hold the broomstick securely in place.

4. Cut two or three pieces of Bubble Wrap to sit inside the neck of the jug to cushion the end of the broomstick and allow the picked fruit to drop comfortably into the bin.

5. Holding the end of the broomstick, raise the bleach jug so that the U-shaped hole in the side is next to the fruit on the tree. Move the jug to position the fruit inside the jug, and then pull downward so that the V-shaped cut in the bottom of the jug captures and breaks the stem, causing the fruit to drop into the container.

HOW IT WORKS

The V shape cut into the bottom of the jug captures the stem of a piece of fruit growing out of reach on a tree. Pulling downward on the broomstick causes the V-shaped plastic to break the stem, capturing the freshly plucked fruit in the jug.

FORBIDDEN FRUIT

- You can also make a homemade fruit picker from a stick and a clean, empty 2-liter soda bottle, a clean, empty coffee can, or a clean, empty tuna fish can attached to a plastic bag.
- To make a net basket to pick fruits from high branches, use a pair of pliers to cut apart a wire clothes hanger, form a hoop approximately 6 inches in diameter, and attach the wire loop to the end of a 10-foot-long wooden pole. Cut off an entire leg from a pair of used, clean panty hose, stretch the open end of the leg around the hoop, and sew it in place.

EVERY TRICK IN THE BOOK
The Versatile Bandana #1

More than just a neckerchief or handkerchief, the bandana boasts innumerable uses. Not only can this colorful cloth be folded to fit in your pocket, but this multipurpose square of fabric can also be a real lifesaver.

- **Baggage Identification.** To make your luggage easier to identify on a baggage carousel, tie a bandana around the handle before you ship your luggage.
- **Bib.** If you're about to feed a child a potentially messy meal, tie a bandana around his or her neck to improvise a bib.
- **Cooling Cloth.** To cool yourself down in hot weather, roll up the bandana, dampen it with water, and wear it tied around your neck.
- **Do-Rag.** Fold the bandana in half diagonally, creating a triangle of fabric. With the point of the triangle facing up, wrap the long side around your head and tie the ends together tightly behind your head. Pull the triangle over the top of your head and tuck the point under the knot. The do-rag works like a hat to protect your head from the heat of the sun and from heat loss in cold weather. A wet do-rag provides evaporative cooling.
- **Dust Mask.** Fold the bandana in half diagonally, cover your nose and mouth with the cloth, and tie the ends around the back of your head to create a dusk mask.
- **First Aid.** In an emergency situation, use a bandana as a bandage, sling, or tourniquet, or to tie a splint.

How to Catch Fish with Soda Bottles

WHAT YOU NEED

- Knife
- Clean, empty 2-liter soda bottle
- Hole puncher
- String (or dental floss)
- Duct tape
- Small stones
- Bread (or other bait)

WHAT TO DO

1. Using a knife or a pair of scissors, cut off the top of the 2-liter soda bottle.
2. Turn the top around and insert it into the bottom section of the bottle so that the mouth of the bottle faces the bottom of the bottle, creating what looks like a funnel. Keep the cut edge of the bottle top and the cut edge of the bottle bottom aligned together.
3. Secure the two pieces of the bottle together by punching holes around the rim and sewing them together with string. Or attach the two rims together with a few strips of duct tape.
4. Attach the end of a long string to one of the holes in the top of the bottle. This string will be used as a mooring line.
5. Insert some small stones to make sure the bottle sinks when placed in the water.
6. Put some bread in the trap and submerge the bottle in the shallow water of a stream, river, or lake, allowing the bottle to fill with water and positioning it to lie horizontally on the bed. Secure the trap in place with some rocks.
7. Tie the end of the string to a bush or tree branch.
8. Let the bottle sit undisturbed until some hapless minnows or small fish swim into the trap.
9. Reel in the string to retrieve the fish trap.
10. Stand the bottle on a flat surface to double as a live bait keeper, until you're ready to use the trapped fish as bait.

HOW IT WORKS

The trap funnels small fish into the bottle, where they remain, unable to figure out how to swim back out of the bottle trap.

A FINE KETTLE OF FISH

The Mediterranean Sea operates like a bottle trap. Fish from the Atlantic Ocean enter the Mediterranean Sea by swimming through the narrow neck of the Strait of Gibraltar (8 miles wide) but have difficulty finding their way out.

EVERY TRICK IN THE BOOK
The Versatile Bandana #2

Here are even more uses for this diverse piece of fabric.

- **Handkerchief.** If you don't have a handkerchief or any tissues, blow your nose into a bandana.
- **Headband.** Fold a bandana in half diagonally, roll it up, and tie it around your head to absorb the beads of sweat from your forehead (and to keep your hair in place).
- **Mask.** In the Wild West, bandits used bandanas, folded in half diagonally and tied around the back of their heads, to cover their faces and mask their identities.
- **Mechanics Glove.** If you need to remove the radiator cap or check the oil, wrap a bandana around your hand to avoid burning yourself or getting oil on your hands.
- **Napkin.** A bandana makes an excellent dinner napkin.
- **Placemat.** Don't have a tablecloth? Spread out a bandana to fancy up that meal at a picnic table.
- **Potholder.** In a pinch, a bandana folded several times works as potholder.
- **Sanitary Napkin.** In an emergency, a bandana folded several times to the appropriate size and shape doubles as a sanitary pad.
- **Toilet Paper.** If you find yourself in an emergency situation, a bandana can come in handy.
- **Towel.** In a tight predicament, you can use a bandana as a small towel.
- **Washcloth.** If you don't have a genuine washcloth, dampen a bandana to do double duty. The thin cotton cloth dries quickly.
- **Water Filter.** To filter sediment and debris from water, pour it through a bandana.

How to Make a Fishing Rod with Dental Floss and a Paper Clip

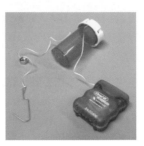

WHAT YOU NEED

- Paper clip
- Dental floss
- Metal washer or nut (for screws or bolts)
- Condom, cork, or clean, empty plastic prescription pill bottle and cap
- Needle (optional)
- Thin but sturdy pole or tree branch, 3 feet in length (optional)

WHAT TO DO

1. Open a paper clip into the shape of the letter S and twist the bottom half of the S perpendicular to the top half.
2. Tie the end of a long strand of dental floss to the top half of the paper clip and twist the loop of metal closed.
3. Tie a metal washer or nut approximately 2 inches above the paper clip to serve as a sinker to weight the hook.
4. Tie a slightly inflated condom, cork, or a sealed, airtight plastic prescription pill bottle to the line at whatever depth you want to suspend the hook and bait. To attach a cork to the line, use a needle to sew the dental floss through the cork, or bore a hole through the cork, run the line through it, and tie it in place. To attach the prescription bottle to the line, open the cap, hold the fishing line across the mouth of the bottle, and snap on and twist the cap.
5. If desired, tie the free end of the line to a 3-foot-long pole or tree branch.

HOW IT WORKS

The float suspends the bait at whatever depth you predetermine, allows the baited hook to float out to deeper waters, and bobs in the water when a fish is on the hook, alerting you to reel in the line.

HOOK. LINE. AND SINKER

- You can also fashion a fishing hook from small thorny branches, plant barbs, bones, bobby pins, or safety pins.
- To make a fishing hook from a thorny branch, cut off a small section of branch with a thorn at one end. Carve a notch around the opposite end of the branch, and tie your line around the notch.

- To construct a treble hook, use wire to attach three open safety pins together, back-to-back.
- To create a gorge hook, tie the fishing line to the center of a toothpick. Turn the toothpick parallel with the fishing line, and bait the entire toothpick. When a fish swallows the bait, the toothpick turns perpendicular to the fishing line, getting stuck inside the fish.
- Wrapping your homemade fishing gear in a small sheet of aluminum foil prevents the line from tangling and the hooks from rusting.
- Assemble a survival fishing kit by wrapping fishing line around a small, empty thread spool; tie the end of the line to a fishing hook; and slip the spool and hook inside a clean, empty, plastic prescription pill bottle, which can be used as a bobber.
- To build a fish scaler, nail metal bottle caps, bottom side up, to a wood block. Rake the bottle caps along the side of the fish in the opposite direction that the scales grow.
- While fishing, store your bait in a leg cut from a pair of clean, used panty hose. Tie the open end of the panty hose leg to a tree branch or fence post for safekeeping.
- Use clean, empty 2 liter soda bottles or a plastic prescription pill bottle, tightly capped, as buoys to mark fishing spots. Tie one end of a string around the neck of the bottle, with the other end tied to a heavy stone to anchor the buoy.
- The best fishing is generally at dawn and dusk. On lakes and ponds, fish generally dwell in the deepest, coolest water or in shaded areas.
- In shallow streams, fish typically congregate in shaded spots under hanging vegetation, logs across the stream, or undercuts of banks. Fish also linger in stagnant pools created by backwashes and behind rocks blocking the current.
- Try to catch several small fish rather than spending all your energy and resources trying to catch a big one.
- If possible, set out several fishing lines to increase your odds of catching something. To do so, cut several lengths of line, tie a hook to each one, bait the hooks, and hang each line from a tree limb extending over the water, allowing the hooks to sink up to 2 feet in the water.

EVERY TRICK IN THE BOOK

The Handy Paper Clip

The paper clip, invented and patented in 1899 by Norwegian inventor Johan Vaaler, boasts a profusion of alternative uses, which, if written on individual index cards, could be held together with—you guessed it—a paper clip.

- **Bookmark.** Simply attach the paper clip to a page to mark your place in a book.
- **Christmas Ornament Hanger.** Open a paper clip into the shape of the letter S to hang an ornament from a Christmas tree.
- **Function Button Activator.** Straighten one end of a paper clip to set the tiny function buttons on a wristwatch or other electronic device.
- **Key Chain.** Attach a shared key to a paper clip, and then hang the paper clip from a nail or hook on the wall.
- **Light Fixture Chain Extension.** Hook together paper clips to extend the length of the chain on a light fixture.
- **Pushpin Adapter.** Open a paper clip into the shape of the letter S and twist the bottom half of the S perpendicular to the top half. Hang one loop from a pushpin on a bulletin board or cubicle wall and hang a small calendar or memo pad from the hook formed by the bottom half of the paper clip.
- **Ring Binder.** To hold papers punched with holes in their tops or sides, simply thread a paper clip through each set of holes.
- **Shrink-Wrap Opener.** Straighten a paper clip to make a tool for breaking open the shrink-wrap on packages.
- **Staple Remover.** Use a straightened paper clip to extract a staple from a bulletin board, stack of papers, or woodwork.
- **Visitor Tag Clip.** Attach a visitor's tag to a shirt pocket, belt, or buttonhole with a paper clip.
- **Zipper Tab.** If you lose a zipper tab, loop a paper clip through the hole in the slider body.

How to Devise a Fishing Net with Panty Hose

WHAT YOU NEED

- Clean, used pair of panty hose
- Y-shaped branch, approximately 1 inch thick
- Needle
- Thread
- Scissors

WHAT TO DO

1. Stretch the waistband of the panty hose over the Y-shaped branch, folding the edge of the waistband back over the branch.
2. Using the needle and thread, sew the edge of the waistband like a hem over the branch.
3. Tie a tight knot in each panty hose leg at the top of each thigh.
4. Using the scissors, cut off each panty hose leg under the knot.

HOW IT WORKS

The tight netting of the panty hose, supported by the frame and handle of the Y-shaped branch, doubles as a fishing net, enabling you to catch small fish or other aquatic animals.

CASTING A WIDER NET

- In "The Peasant's Wise Daughter," a story collected by the Brothers Grimm in *Grimm's Fairy Tales*, a king instructs a peasant girl to come to him "not clothed, not naked...." The peasant girl cleverly wraps herself in fishnet.
- Fishnet stockings arrived in America in 1908 from Paris, France.
- Pin-up girls—including Bettie Page, Marilyn Monroe, Anita Ekberg, Jane Wyman, Zsa Zsa Gabor, and Brigitte Bardot—frequently wore fishnet stockings in their pin-up photos.
- With the advent of the miniskirt in the 1960s, fishnet stockings gained widespread popularity, and a decade later, women in the punk rock subculture wore fishnet stockings to downplay the sexiness of the legwear. In the 1990s, women in the Goth subculture embraced fishnet stockings as a part of their black attire. Women also wore fishnet stockings beneath torn jeans, and ultimately fishnet stockings became acceptable legwear under knee-length skirts.

How to Build a One-Man Tent with Trash Bags

WHAT YOU NEED
- 2 or 3 contractor-grade 45-gallon (or 55-gallon) plastic trash bags
- Knife or scissors

WHAT TO DO
1. Insert your feet into one of the trash bags, pull the top of the bag up around your waist, and secure the string tie firmly around your waist.
2. Using a knife or pair of scissors, cut an opening in the closed end of the other trash bag at a 90-degree angle along a seam about 5 inches below one corner. The hole should be just large enough to allow you to pass your head through it.
3. Place the trash bag over your head until your face aligns with the hole.
4. Pull the string tie shut from inside the bag.
5. To make a mattress (or insulation pad), stuff a third trash bag with dry leaves, tie it securely shut, and sit or lie on it.

HOW IT WORKS
The trash bag creates a lightweight, waterproof emergency shelter. The hole in the bag allows you to breathe and lets the water vapor in your perspiration and exhaled breath escape from the plastic bag, rather than creating condensation on the inside walls of the bag, making you wet. The mattress provides insulation against the cold ground and padding for comfort.

GIMME SHELTER
- Convert a plastic trash bag into exceptional impromptu rain gear. Simply cut a hole in the middle of the bottom of a plastic trash bag and pull it over your head to cover your body with the waterproof plastic.
- In a pinch, use a trash bag as a poor man's sleeping bag. For insulation, stuff the waterproof bag with dry grasses or crumpled-up sheets of newspaper.

EVERY TRICK IN THE BOOK

The Power of the Shower Curtain

A clean, used plastic shower curtain is a free sheet of heavy-duty plastic capable of protecting almost anything. Clean the shower curtain by wiping it down with a sponge dampened with full-strength vinegar. To clean mildew from the shower curtain, place the curtain in your washing machine along with several towels, add 2 cups white vinegar.

- **Apron.** Using a pair of scissors, cut an apron pattern from your shower curtain, with a loop at the top (to go over your head) and ties at the waist.
- **Emergency Shelter.** In an emergency, use a shower curtain to create an emergency shelter, such as a tent, tarp, or lean-to.
- **Ground Cloth.** Use a shower curtain as a ground cloth under a tent or sleeping bag. The thick plastic shower curtain prevents sharp rocks or sticks from tearing a hole in the tent floor or poking your body. The waterproof shower curtain also stops ground moisture from seeping through your tent floor.
- **Rain Gear.** To make a rain poncho, fold a plastic shower curtain in half, and cut a hole for your head to fit through in the middle of the fold. Drape the shower curtain over your head.
- **Tablecloth.** Drape a clean, plastic shower curtain over a picnic table or the ground to create an instant, waterproof tablecloth or picnic blanket.
- **Tarp.** Drape a plastic shower curtain over bicycles, barbecue grills, or a woodpile to protect them from rain or snow.
- **Tote Bag.** To convert a plastic shower curtain into a bag for carrying or storing beachwear, laundry, toys, or other items, fold the curtain in half with the holes for the shower curtain hooks folded against each other. Leaving the holes for the top of the bag, cut the curtain to the desired size. Sew the bottom and side closed. Turn the bag inside out to create clean seams, and thread a rope through the holes to create a tie cord.
- **Windshield Cover.** To avoid scraping ice off your windshield, use scissors to cut a broad sheet of plastic from a shower curtain to cover the windshield and overhang each side. Place the plastic sheet over the windshield, and close the car doors over the edges of the plastic to hold it in place. When you're ready to drive, brush off any snow and peel off the plastic for an ice-free windshield. To make a more elaborate windshield cover, use a sewing machine to hem the plastic with strong magnets inside the hems.

How to Assemble a Tube Tent with Trash Bags

WHAT YOU NEED

- 3 or 4 contractor-grade 45- or 55-gallon plastic trash bags
- Knife or scissors
- Duct tape
- Rope, approximately 15 feet in length
- Logs or stones

WHAT TO DO

1. Cut the bottom seams of some plastic contractor trash bags with a knife or pair of scissors (four bags if using 45-gallon bags; three bags if using 55-gallon bags).
2. Attach the open ends of each bag together with duct tape to make one long plastic tube roughly 7 feet long.
3. Tie one end of the rope to a tree, approximately 2 feet off the ground.
4. Feed the free end of the rope through the bottomless trash bag.
5. Tie the free end of the rope to a second tree at the same height as the first end of the rope and far enough away to fully open the trash bag to its full length. Tie the rope taut. Make sure the rope runs perpendicular to the direction of the wind; otherwise the wind will blow through the tube tent.
6. Extend the bottom sides of the plastic tube to form a triangle tent by laying two long, thin logs inside the tube along the length of each side. (Or place large stones along both sides of the tent floor.) If you prefer to use rope to pull out and tie down the sides of the tent, place a small object (such as a smooth stone, acorn, or other marble-sized object) inside the corner of the plastic and push it toward the outside of the tent to form a protrusion. Tie a slipknot in one end of a short piece of rope, place the loop around the protrusion, pull the loop tight, and peg the free end of the rope to the ground.

HOW IT WORKS

The waterproof tent—a large tube hung on a rope and made from a sheet of plastic—provides sufficient space for relative comfort and adequate protection from the elements.

A ROOF OVER YOUR HEAD

- To make a mattress (or insulation pad), stuff another trash bag with dry leaves, tie it securely shut, and place it on the floor of the tube tent. The mattress provides insulation against the cold ground and padding for comfort.
- To fashion an insulated comforter, stuff another trash bag with dry leaves, tie it securely shut, and use it as a blanket.
- For a pillow, inflate a large ziplock storage bag with air (or stuff if with dry leaves) and zip it securely shut. Or fill the plastic bag with Styrofoam peanuts, squeeze out some of the air, and seal it shut.
- Another way to make a tent: tie a rope taut between two trees, drape a tarp over it, and use short ropes to tie out the sides using stakes.

EVERY TRICK IN THE BOOK
Raising the Stakes

Several household items make excellent substitutes for tent stakes:

- **Clothespins**
- **Cutlery**
- **Knitting needles (size 8 or above)**
- **Paintbrushes**
- **Wood spoons**
- **Wooden dowels (cut into 6-inch lengths)**

If you don't have stakes or any of the above objects, use sticks or tie each stake line to a large rock.

How to Create an Emergency Toilet with Kitty Litter

WHAT YOU NEED
- 5-gallon plastic bucket
- Garbage bag
- Kitty litter
- Toilet seat (unscrewed from your household toilet) or a snap-on toilet seat (available at prepper supply stores)
- Hand sanitizer

WHAT TO DO
1. Line the inside of the bucket with a garbage bag.
2. Pour 3 cups of kitty litter into the garbage bag.
3. Place the toilet seat on top of the rim of the bucket.
4. After defecating in the emergency toilet, cover the feces with another 2 or 3 cups of kitty litter.
5. Before each use, scoop out the clumps.
6. Wash your hands after each use with hand sanitizer (or soap and water, if available).

HOW IT WORKS
Each time you use your emergency toilet, the kitty litter will desiccate the feces, which can be scooped out and placed in a double garbage bag labeled HUMAN WASTE for proper disposal by sanitation authorities once service is reestablished.

A ROYAL FLUSH
- Store a roll of toilet paper in a clean, empty coffee can with a lid. The waterproof can keeps the toilet paper dry.
- A clean, empty Gatorade or juice bottle makes an excellent urine bottle for camping or travel.
- A clean, empty 3-pound coffee can with a lid makes a basic, primitive chamber pot that should be discreetly emptied after each use or first thing in the morning.

How to Construct a Washing Machine with a Plunger

WHAT YOU NEED
- 5-gallon bucket with lid
- Drill with 1-inch bit
- Utility knife
- Plunger
- Detergent
- Water (ideally warm)

WHAT TO DO

1. Drill a hole in the center of the lid.
2. Using a utility knife, cut three to six holes around the perimeter of the plunger.
3. Pour detergent in the bucket (25 percent of whatever amount you use in your regular wash load).
4. Fill the bucket halfway full with water (warm water works better).

5. Place your dirty clothes in the bucket, allowing the water level to rise to fill three-quarters of the bucket.
6. Insert the free end of the plunger pole through the hole in the bottom of the lid and snap the lid on the bucket.
7. Pump the plunger up and down, as if you were churning butter, for 3 to 5 minutes.
8. Remove the lid and pour out the soapy water, leaving the clothes in the bucket.

9. Fill the bucket three-quarters full with clean water, replace the plunger and lid, and continue pumping the plunger for the rinse cycle.
10. Repeat steps 8 and 9 above for the final rinse cycle.
11. Remove the lid, pour out the rinse water (you can use it to water a flower bed or garden), wring out the clothes, and hang them on a clothesline to dry in the sun.

HOW IT WORKS

The pumping action of the plunger works like the agitator in your washing machine.

ALL WASHED UP

- To give the plunger a longer handle, unscrew the handle and replace it with a broomstick.
- To keep the plunger handle straight while pumping (to prevent water from splashing through the hole in the lid), cut off the bottom of a plastic prescription pill bottle. Insert the bottle into the hole in the lid to create a gasket and glue it in place with epoxy.
- A clean, empty glass jar or a large coffee can makes a miniature washing machine for small, delicate items like gloves, panty hose, and silks. Place the garment in the jar, fill the jar three-quarters full with tepid water, and add a few drops of soap. Replace the lid securely and shake the jar vigorously for 5 minutes. Rinse well, wring gently, and hang up the item to dry.

How to Make Soap with Ashes and Fat

WHAT YOU NEED

- Spoon
- 6 pounds of hardened, leftover cooking fat (collected in an empty tin can after cooking and refrigerated)
- Large stainless steel pot
- Water
- Knife
- Drill with ¼-inch bit
- 3 clean, empty coffee cans, one smaller than the others
- Wood ashes (from a fireplace or campfire)
- Safety goggles
- Rubber gloves
- Uncooked egg
- Cooking thermometer
- Measuring cup
- 36½ ounces of the purest water possible (rainwater, distilled water, or demineralized water)
- Glass bowl
- Wooden spoon
- Muffin tin
- Waxed paper

WHAT TO DO

1. Scoop the fat into a large stainless steel pot with an equal amount of water.
2. Heat until the water boils and the fat melts.
3. Remove the pot from the heat and let it sit overnight so the fat cools and solidifies as a layer on top of the water.
4. With a knife, cut the fat into chunks and scrape any debris from the bottom of each chunk.
5. If the chunks of fat retain any food particles or debris, repeat steps 1 though 4 above.
6. Drill holes in the bottom of the smaller coffee can.
7. Fill the can two-thirds full with wood ashes.
8. Suspend the can of ashes over the larger can.
9. Wearing safety goggles and rubber gloves, fill the upper can with hot water, letting it leech through the ashes and drain into the bottom can. The resulting liquid is lye solution, a caustic chemical that can cause severe burns. ***If you accidentally get lye on your skin,*** flush the area with white vinegar and wash thoroughly with soap and

water. *If you get lye in your eye,* flush with water and seek immediate medical attention.

10. When all the water drains from the top can, carefully pour the lye solution from the bottom can into the top can and let it drain through a second time into the third can.

11. Carefully place the raw egg (unbroken in its shell) in the lye solution. If the egg sinks, the concentration of lye in the solution is too low; pour the solution through the ashes again to increase the concentration— until the egg floats in the lye solution.

12. Melt the 6 pounds of fat in a large stainless steel pot and, using a cooking thermometer, let the melted fat cool to 130°F.

13. Pour 36½ ounces of the purest water possible into a glass bowl.

14. Wearing safety goggles and rubber gloves, gradually add 13 ounces of lye to the water in the glass bowl, stirring with the wooden spoon. *Never pour the water into the lye.* Doing so can cause the mixture to explode, blowing very corrosive lye water everywhere.

15. The lye and water will generate a lot of heat. Using a cooking thermometer, let the lye water cool to 110°F.

16. If the temperature of the fat reaches 130°F before the lye cools to 110°F, speed the cooling of the lye by setting the glass bowl in a pan of cool water a few inches deep.

17. Stir the fat in one direction (either clockwise or counterclockwise) and very slowly pour the lye water into it as you continue stirring.

18. Continue stirring until the soap solution attains the consistency of honey (roughly 20 minutes).

19. Pour the liquid soap into the compartments in the muffin tin.

20. Let the tin sit undisturbed for 24 hours.

21. Remove the soap from the tin and wrap the muffin-shaped bars of soap in waxed paper.

22. Store the wrapped soap in a cool place for three weeks so it cures and hardens.

HOW IT WORKS

When appropriate amounts of lye, water, and fat are mixed together, a chemical reaction called *saponification* results, meaning the fat fuses with the alkali to form soap.

IN A LATHER

Lye, a caustic alkali made from wood ashes, burns through clothes, rubber gloves, skin, and eyes.

How to Build a Solar-Powered Shower with a Trash Bag

WHAT YOU NEED

- Plastic trash bag
- Water
- Rope, 20 feet long
- Scissors

WHAT TO DO

1. Fill a black plastic trash bag with water.
2. Pull the tie cord to secure the bag shut.
3. Tie the end of the rope to the top of the bag. Toss the other over a tall, solid tree branch and hoist the bag a foot off the ground.
4. Tie the free end of the rope to the trunk of the tree or a low branch to secure the trash bag in place.
5. Let the sun heat the bag of water for several hours.
6. Untie the free end of the rope, hoist the bag a few inches above your head, and retie the free end of the rope to the trunk of the tree or a low branch to secure the trash bag in place.
7. Gather your soap and towel and remove your clothes (or put on a bathing suit).
8. Using the scissors, snip off a small bottom corner of the bag (or poke a few holes in the plastic bag).
9. Stand under the stream of warm water to take your shower.

HOW IT WORKS

The black plastic bag, when exposed to sunlight, converts light energy to heat energy. The bag also traps and retains the heat, which gradually heats the water inside the bag to roughly 100°F.

SQUEAKY CLEAN

- In a pinch, a compressed-air garden sprayer can be used as a shower. (Never utilize a used compressed-air insecticide sprayer as a shower.)
- To heat water, save empty bleach jugs and 2-liter soda bottles. Paint the clean, empty jugs and bottles black with tempera paint and fill them with water. Set them in the sun in the morning. By late afternoon, the water will be hot enough to use for washing dishes or bathing.

- To make a portable changing room, attach an opaque shower curtain to a Hula Hoop using standard shower rings, and then hang the Hula Hoop from a tree branch or have someone hold it in place while you change.
- Drop a bar of soap in a leg cut from an old pair of panty hose, tie a knot to secure the bar of soap in the foot, and tie the other end of the leg to an outdoor water spigot or tree branch. The panty hose keeps the bar of soap clean and accessible.
- Can't get a hot shower in the wilderness? Pack baby wipes in a ziplock storage bag to give yourself a quick sponge bath when you're feeling filthy.

How to Fashion a Signal Mirror from a Used CD

WHAT YOU NEED
- CD (or DVD)

WHAT TO DO
1. Hold the CD in one hand. Outstretch your free arm and spread your index finger and middle finger to form the letter V.
2. Position the V so that you can see the target (an airplane, helicopter, or ground vehicle) between your fingers.
3. Hold the CD with the shiny side facing the sun, and looking through the hole in the center of the CD, reflect the sunlight onto your two outstretched fingers so that the reflected light passes between the V.
4. Slowly move your fingers to capture your target between the V, keeping the reflected light from the CD passing through the V.
5. With the target and reflected light between the V, tilt the mirror back and forth—flashing the reflected sunlight at the target.
6. Keep the bright light focused on the target as you tilt the mirror.

HOW IT WORKS
The shiny side of the CD or DVD sends signals by reflecting sunlight. Each inch of mirror diameter reflects sunlight an average of 10 miles. Thus, a 4½-inch-diameter mirror should reflect sunlight an average of 45 miles, but the circular groove and microscopic bumps used to store data on a CD disrupt the mirror's smooth surface, causing diffraction and interference—limiting the CD's reflective ability.

GET THE MESSAGE?
- Cut the CD into a rectangular shape and smooth the sharp edges with sandpaper (or cover them with duct tape) to make a signal mirror that fits into a survival kit fashioned from an Altoids tin.
- Under normal conditions, light reflected from a signal mirror can be seen for up to 30 miles.
- The distance a mirror signal can be seen depends on the clearness of the sky, the length of uninterrupted sight, and the size of the mirror used.
- A signal mirror is considered one of the most underrated and useful instruments for signaling for help.

- Any reflective object can be used to reflect the sun's rays, including polished canteen cups, a makeup compact mirror, belt buckles, a tin can lid, a rearview mirror removed from a car, aluminum foil, a space blanket, or the hologram on a credit card.
- By holding a piece of cardboard in front of the CD to interrupt the flashes, you can send short and long flashes, delivering Morse code messages. Three short flashes of light, followed by three long flashes of light, followed by three short flashes of light signal SOS.

EVERY TRICK IN THE BOOK

Making the Rounds with CDs and DVDs

CDs and DVDs may be going the way of the eight-track tape, but those shiny disks have far more alternative uses than their archaic audio ancestor.

- **Candle Holder.** Adhere a candle in the center of the CD with the shiny side up. The disk reflects the light from the lit candle, creating a beautiful sparkle.
- **Car Stopper.** Tie one end of a string through the hole in the disk, and attach the other end of the string to your garage ceiling so the disk touches the windshield of your properly parked car. Now, whenever you pull into the garage, you'll know to stop the car when the disk touches the windshield—without hitting the wall and assured that the car sits far enough inside the garage door.
- **Deer Chaser.** Use string (or dental floss) to hang the shiny disks from tree branches, fences, or a taut line strung across a garden. The flashes of sunlight from the disks frighten away deer.
- **Driveway Reflector.** Attach a disk to the top of a wooden stake to create an inexpensive driveway reflector.
- **Mini-Frisbee.** Toss the disk just like a flying saucer toy. Use a blow-dryer to heat the disk and bend it into more unusual aerodynamic shapes.
- **Pull Chain.** To make a pull chain in a dark closet or attic easier to spot, attach a disk to the end of the chain. The disk reflects even the dimmest light, making it simple to locate.

How to Put Together a Baby Mobile with Used CDs

WHAT YOU NEED

- 2 wire clothes hangers
- Dental floss
- Duct tape (optional)
- Several CDs or DVDs

WHAT TO DO

1. Place the two wire clothes hangers together and then pivot them at the center to form an X with the bases of the hanger wires.

2. Gently twist one of the hanger loops perpendicular to its body so that the hanger loop lies flat against the second hanger loop.

3. Using dental floss (or duct tape), secure the hangers together at the X formed by the bases and at the apex where the two triangles meet.

4. With different lengths of dental floss, tie the CDs or DVDs securely to the crossbars, allowing them to dangle at various heights but making sure the mobile remains balanced.

5. Hook the hanger loop to a tree branch or use dental floss to suspend the loop, above a baby's head and well out of reach of the youngster.

HOW IT WORKS

The mirrored surfaces of the CDs or DVDs reflect light, and the combined effect of diffraction and interference caused by the circular grooves in the disks create rainbow patterns and a visual treat for infants.

How to Make Snow Goggles with a Cereal Box

WHAT YOU NEED
- Clean, empty cereal box
- Scissors or knife
- Dental floss or shoelace
- Charcoal (optional)

WHAT TO DO
1. Open the cereal box into a flat sheet of cardboard.
2. Using the scissors or a knife, cut a 3-inch-tall rectangular strip of cardboard the width of your face.
3. Cut two slots for eyeholes (2 inches wide by ⅛ inch high).
4. In the center of the cardboard strip, cut a slit on each side of the nose—from the bottom edge to the midline.
5. Fold the nose flap up and, holding the rectangle to your face, bend the sides of the flap against the sides of your nose.
6. Cut a hole near each end of the mask, and tie dental floss or a shoelace through the holes to make a head strap.
7. Smear charcoal (or soot from a wood fire) under your eyes to protect against sun glare.

HOW IT WORKS
Snow and ice intensify the reflected ultraviolet rays of the sun. Exposing unprotected eyes to this fierce glare can cause snow blindness—red, watering, sore eyes accompanied by intense headaches. Wearing high-quality sunglasses or even a pair of crude goggles fashioned from cardboard or tree bark helps prevent snow blindness by blocking the intensified ultraviolet rays.

A SIGHT FOR SORE EYES

- You can also make a pair of snow goggles with duct tape. Cut a 1-foot-long strip of duct tape and fold it in half lengthwise, adhering the tape to itself. Using a knife or scissors, cut one long slot (4 inches wide by ⅛ inch tall) in the middle of the folded duct tape. Use a long strip of duct tape, folded in half widthwise, to fashion a strap to wear the goggles around your head.

- In a pinch, you can make a snow visor from a space blanket. Cut a strip of the space blanket, and wrap it around your head as a pair of goggles. The see-through material doubles as sunglasses.

- If you're desperate, fashion snow goggles by peeling a wide strip of paper bark from the trunk of a white birch tree. Then follow the directions above for making snow goggles from a cereal box.

- To treat snow blindness, rest your eyes, ideally in a dark place, or blindfold yourself, until the irritation subsides.

How to Produce Snowshoes from Tennis Rackets

WHAT YOU NEED
- 2 tennis rackets
- 4 bungee cords

WHAT TO DO
1. Wearing shoes, stand on the tennis rackets.
2. Wrap a bungee cord around your left foot just below the toes and then secure the hooks into the weave of the racket along each side of your foot.
3. Wrap a second bungee cord around your ankle and then secure it into the weave of the racket behind your foot.
4. Repeat steps 2 and 3 for your right foot.
5. To walk on snow, lift one foot slightly and slide the inner edge of the tennis racket over the inner edge of the other tennis racket.

HOW IT WORKS
The surface area of the tennis racquets distributes the wearer's weight over a greater area of snow, putting less pressure (or pounds per square inch) on the snow, which prevents the person from sinking in the snow.

FLAKE OUT
- If you don't have bungee cords, use rope to secure your shoes to the tennis racket. Place the middle of the rope across the top of your foot, just below the toes, and feed the ends through the weave of the racket alongside the foot. Feed the ends back up through the weave on both sides behind the heel, pull tightly, and tie the ends around the ankle.
- Slim people, putting less pressure on snow, can get by using a smaller pair of snowshoes than heavier-set people, whose weight puts more pressure on snow.
- Packed snow takes more pressure than freshly fallen, fluffy snow.
- An old tennis racket can be utilized to beat carpets during spring-cleaning.
- In the 1960 movie *The Apartment*, C. C. Baxter (Jack Lemmon) uses a tennis racket to strain cooked spaghetti.

6

FIRST AID EMERGENCIES

You're lost in the woods, suffering from an inexplicable toothache. You stumble through poison ivy, break your arm, and get wounded by a bullet. All you've got in your backpack are Tabasco sauce, nail polish remover, a pair of panty hose, and tampons. Are you totally screwed?

How to Make a Signal Whistle with a Bottle Cap

WHAT YOU NEED
- Cap from a soda or water bottle
- Patience

WHAT TO DO

1. Form two fists with your thumbs resting on top of your index fingers.
2. Position your two fists together with the flesh of palms against each other and the sides of your thumbs alongside each other.
3. Place the bottle cap (with the hollow side facing up) on your bent index fingers and hold it in place with your thumbs, creating a V shape between the top of your thumbs over the bottle cap. Make sure the bottle cap is totally sealed by your thumbs with the exception of the V shape.
4. Press your lower lip against the bent joint of your thumbs with your upper lip resting on top of the first joint.
5. Blow hard across the top of your thumbs, adjusting the angle until you produce a loud whistling sound.

HOW IT WORKS
Blowing air into the cap creates a high-pressure chamber. The air escaping through the small V shape formed by your fingers makes a whistling noise.

CLOSE CALL
- Cut off the bottom of a milk or bleach jug to make a megaphone to call for help.
- A metal whistle delivers a louder blast than whistles made from plastic, which deadens sound.

How to Make a Signal Whistle with a Soda Can

WHAT YOU NEED

- Tin snips, a knife, or scissors
- Soda can

WHAT TO DO

1. Using tin snips, a knife, or scissors, cut the top and bottom off the can and discard those pieces. **Be careful not to cut yourself** on the sharp edges of the aluminum.

2. Cut the remaining aluminum cylinder from top to bottom.

3. Flatten the aluminum rectangle.

4. Cut a rectangular strip of aluminum 5 inches long and ¾ inch wide.

5. Snip a 1½ inch piece from the end of the 5-inch-long strip.

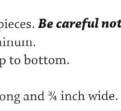

6. Place the short rectangle (1½ inches by ¾ inch) over one end of the long rectangle, crosswise and centered.

7. Fold the extended ends of the short rectangle around the long rectangle and press firmly so the short piece stays in place.

8. At the line formed where the short piece overlaps the long rectangle, fold the long rectangle down to form a 90-degree angle.

9. Holding the free end of the long rectangle, bend the long rectangle back up and around to the top of the fold, forming the cylinder of a round whistle—without any sides.

10. Insert the small tip of the tin snips, knife, or scissors in the space at the edge where you wrapped the short rectangle around the long rectangle. Twist the blade slightly to enlarge the gap just enough so you can blow air through it.

11. Hold the whistle between your thumb on one side and your index and middle finger on the other side—using the flesh of your fingertips as

the sides of the whistle. If your fingers are too small to seal the sides, hold the whistle between your palms.

12. Position the top to create a small slot between the fold and the edge of the long rectangle.

13. *Being careful not to cut your lips* on the sharp edges of the aluminum, blow through the gap you enlarged between the short and long rectangles.

HOW IT WORKS

Air blown through the mouthpiece of the whistle hits the slot, which slices the airflow in two. The top portion is deflected upward, creating whirling vortexes that cause vibrations in the air above the slot. The lower portion enters the whistle chamber, swirls back up through the slot, and intensifies the vibrations caused by the whirling vortexes.

SLICK AS A WHISTLE

- A ball inside a whistle chamber alternately blocks and unblocks part of the slot, producing a warbling tone.
- Certain pitches of sound sometimes seem louder than others at the same decibel level. A high-pitched whistle might seem louder than a low-pitched whistle with a higher decibel rating.
- In 1878, British toolmaker Joseph Hudson fashioned a brass whistle to be used by the referee, in place of waving a handkerchief, during a match at the Nottingham Forest Soccer Club.
- In 1883, the London police advertised for an idea to replace a police officer's hand rattle. Hudson invented a light, compact whistle that could be held in the mouth and which produced two loud, discordant tones. A year later, Hudson added a small ball to the whistle chamber, producing a trilling sound.
- The ball inside of pea whistles is generally made of cork.

How to Stop Bleeding from a Bullet Wound with Tampons

WHAT YOU NEED

- Unscented maxi pads (or disposable diapers)
- Duct tape
- Triple antibiotic ointment (optional)
- Tampon
- Condom (optional)
- Bandana (or strip of cloth torn from a shirt or bedsheet)

WHAT TO DO

1. Do not attempt to remove the bullet from the wound. Doing so can cause serious bleeding, infection, or further damage. If the bullet has penetrated through the body, you'll need to plug the holes to stop the bleeding and stabilize the victim.
2. Elevate the injury higher than the heart, if possible. Doing so reduces blood pressure in the limb and slows the bleeding.
3. For an injured limb, use a maxi pad to apply firm, continuous pressure on the bleeding wound for 5 to 10 minutes. (If you don't have a maxi pad, use a disposable diaper.) If the maxi pad becomes soaked with blood, place a second one on top of the first and reapply pressure. Removing the first pad can disrupt the clotting of the blood.
4. When 10 minutes has elapsed, slowly release the pressure to check to see if the bleeding has stopped.
5. If the bleeding has stopped and you're headed to an emergency room, do not clean the wound. Apply a clean maxi pad (or diaper) and secure it in place with duct tape. If the bleeding has not stopped, repeat step 3 above for 15 minutes. If you're unable to get to a hospital immediately, flush the wound with water and smear it with a triple antibiotic ointment before applying a clean maxi pad.

6. If the bullet wound won't stop bleeding, as a last resort carefully unwrap a tampon, and use the applicator to insert the sterile cotton tampon into the bullet wound to plug the heavy bleeding. To improvise surgical gloves, wear a condom on your hand or around several fingers.

7. Secure the tampon in place by tying a bandana (or strip of cloth torn from a shirt or bedsheet) around the affected body part. (Or cover the tampon with a maxi pad, held in place with duct tape.)

8. Seek immediate medical attention.

HOW IT WORKS

Used as a compress, a maxi pad made from absorbent Cellucotton helps stop bleeding. Inserted into a bullet wound, a tampon absorbs blood, expands, and fills the cavity created by the bullet. Note that ***removing a tampon from inside a wound can present difficulty for doctors***, because the blood clots in and around it.

BITE THE BULLET

- In 1914, Kimberly-Clark developed Cellucotton, the material used in maxi pads, as substitute for surgical cotton during World War I.
- You can improvise an adhesive bandage from a cotton ball, tissue, or paper towel held in place with a strip of duct tape.
- Carry maxi pads and tampons in your first aid kit as sterile and absorbent dressings for wounds.
- As far back as the Vietnam War, army medics have carried tampons in their medical kits for use in combat to treat wounds.
- In Iraq, US medics used tampons to temporarily plug bullet holes in the wounded.

How to Recover from Diarrhea with Sugar, Salt, and Lemon Juice

WHAT YOU NEED

- 3 teaspoons of sugar
- 1 teaspoon of salt
- 2 teaspoons of lemon juice
- Tall glass of water
- Spoon

WHAT TO DO

1. Mix the sugar, salt, and lemon juice in the glass of water. Stir well.
2. Drink the entire solution.

HOW IT WORKS

Drinking plenty of fluids during a bout of diarrhea is essential to avoiding dehydration. This homemade rehydration solution replaces the glucose, minerals, and vitamin C being flushed out of your body.

WHEN ALL HELL BREAKS LOOSE

- Common causes of diarrhea include viruses, food or water contaminated with bacteria or parasites, medications (most commonly antibiotics), lactose intolerance, fructose, or artificial sweeteners.
- In most cases, diarrhea clears up within a couple of days without any treatment.
- Diarrhea that lasts for weeks can signal a serious disorder, such as inflammatory bowel disease, Crohn's disease, colitis, or irritable bowel syndrome.
- Diarrhea causes the body to lose significant amounts of water and salts. To prevent dehydration, drink plenty of water and fruit juice (not apple or pear, which contain high amounts of sorbitol sugar, which can worsen diarrhea). Fruit juice helps maintain your electrolyte levels, and eating soups or chicken bouillon replaces lost sodium.
- Diarrhea helps purge harmful bacteria or a parasite from your digestive system.
- The best treatment for quick recovery from diarrhea is to let it clear up by itself.

EVERY TRICK IN THE BOOK

Running Amok

To put a cork in the bottle, try one of these tips.

- **Apple Cider Vinegar.** To subdue diarrhea caused by a bacterial infection, drink two tablespoons of apple cider vinegar added to a glass of water. The antibiotic properties of apple cider vinegar combat the bacteria, and the pectin may soothe intestinal spasms.
- **Applesauce.** To tame diarrhea, eat applesauce. The pectin in the applesauce is a soluble fiber that absorbs fluid in your intestine and helps solidify soft bowel movements. Applesauce also contains malic acid and quercetin, which help inhibit harmful bacteria in your stomach.
- **Chicken Bouillon.** To replace the liquids, salts, and minerals depleted by diarrhea, eat chicken bouillon.
- **Coca-Cola.** Drinking flat Coca-Cola helps settle your queasy stomach. Pharmacies sell cola syrup that can be taken in small doses to relieve nausea. The concentrated sugars are believed to relax the gastrointestinal tract. Letting the bubbles out of the soda prevents the carbonation from further upsetting your stomach.
- **Coconut.** Eating 2 teaspoons of coconut flakes helps cure diarrhea.
- **Gatorade.** To refortify your body with liquid and electrolytes, drink Gatorade to quickly replace essential nutrients and minerals, preventing muscle spasms in your stomach.
- **Honey.** To cure diarrhea, mix 4 tablespoons of honey into a cup of hot water. Let it cool and drink. A 1985 study conducted in South Africa and reported in the *British Medical Journal* showed that honey shortens the duration of diarrhea in patients with bacterial gastroenteritis caused by *Salmonella*, *Shigella*, and *E. coli*. (Do not feed honey to infants under one year of age. Honey often carries a benign strain of *C. botulinum*, and an infant's immune system requires 12 months to develop to fight off disease and infection.)
- **Rice.** To get diarrhea under control, eat small portions of plain, white rice. Rice binds the bowels, creating healthy stools.
- **Yogurt.** To ease diarrhea, eat a cup of yogurt. The beneficial *Lactobacillus acidophilus* (probiotics) in yogurt assists the helpful bacteria in your colon that aid digestion.

How to Disinfect a Knife Wound with Mouthwash

WHAT YOU NEED
- Listerine mouthwash (original formula)
- Maxi pads
- Coat or blanket

WHAT TO DO
1. If the knife remains in the victim's body, ***do not attempt to remove or move the object***. Doing so could cause rapid bleeding out, internal tissue damage, or a sucking chest wound (a hole that pulls air into the chest cavity leading to a collapsed lung).
2. Help the victim to lie down, and elevate the feet 6 to 8 inches to keep blood concentrated around the major organs.
3. Elevate the injury higher than the heart if possible. Doing so reduces blood pressure in the limb and slows the bleeding.
4. Saturate the knife wound with Listerine mouthwash (original formula). Pour the Listerine over the wound. Do not scrub. The alcohol in the Listerine will sting.
5. Pack the wound by straddling the knife with maxi pads to stop the bleeding. Do not press on the knife or along the edge of the wound.
6. If the knife wound continues bleeding, press the nearest pressure point above the wound for roughly 1 minute. Pressure points are located inside the wrists, on the inner side of the arms halfway between the elbow and shoulder, and on the inside of the thighs just below the groin.
7. Stabilize the knife by placing maxi pads or clean cloth around the knife to prevent it from moving.
8. To treat shock, wrap a coat or blanket around the victim, without disturbing the knife.
9. Seek immediate medical attention.

HOW IT WORKS

Listerine works as an astringent when poured on a laceration. Listerine is also an analgesic, instantly relieving the pain of an exposed nerve for a considerable length of time. Developed by Dr. Joseph Lawrence in 1857 as a safe and effective antiseptic for use in surgical procedures, Listerine is also an antibacterial.

CLEAN-CUT

- Substitutes for antibacterial ointment include honey or sugar. Both honey and sugar are hygroscopic, meaning they absorb moisture from wounds, making the wound an inhospitable environment for bacteria and sealing out contaminants. To prevent infection, coat the wound with honey or sugar. Honey dries to form a unique bandage. If the sugar turns into a runny glaze (indicating loss of its hygroscopic ability and bacteria-killing ability), clean up the substance and reapply the sugar.
- In a pinch, use a clean Pampers disposable diaper as a compress to stop a knife wound from bleeding.
- Applying Purell Instant Hand Sanitizer disinfects a wound and helps stop the bleeding. The ethyl alcohol in the gel is an antiseptic. Or pour vodka over the wound. The alcohol disinfects the wound.
- In the first century, the ancient Greek physician Dioscorides used sage to stop wounds from bleeding. To do so, simply sprinkle ground sage on the laceration.
- To protect a cut from infection, sprinkle ground cloves on the laceration. The eugenol in the cloves doubles as an antiseptic and a pain reliever, numbing the wound.
- If you're unable to wash a minor wound, lick it with your tongue. A 2008 report by scientists from The Netherlands found that histatin, a small protein in saliva known to kill bacteria, greatly speeds the healing of wounds. This finding explains why animals lick their wounds and why wounds in the mouth heal much faster than flesh wounds.

How to Make Knee Pads with a Bra

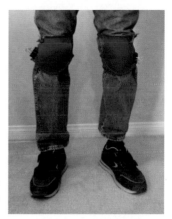

WHAT YOU NEED
- Scissors or knife
- Padded underwire bra
- Duct tape or binder clips

WHAT TO DO
1. Using scissors or a knife, cut a padded underwire bra in half between the two cups.
2. Cut the end of the spaghetti strap from the back strap.
3. Place the right cup over the right knee and the left cup over the left knee so the support wire rests below the kneecap.

4. Wrap the back strap around the upper calf and attach the free end to the cup with duct tape or a binder clip.
5. Wrap the spaghetti strap around the lower thigh and attach the free end to the cup with duct tape or a binder clip.

HOW IT WORKS
The padding in the bra cups cushions your knees.

ON BENDED KNEE
- You can also make knee pads with maxi pads. Simply remove the convenient adhesive strip and adhere the maxi pads to your knees to create instant knee pads. You can also adhere them to the knees of your pants and secure them in place with duct tape.
- Women at the Church of Guadalupe in Mexico City often wear maxi pads on their knees to pray.
- Knees get injured from sports activities, falls, automobile accidents, overuse, daily wear and tear, kneeling, and squatting.
- If you're overweight, losing excess weight reduces the stress placed on your knees exponentially. Every pound you weigh places roughly 6 pounds of pressure on your knees.

- To relieve knee pain, sit down and prop up your injured leg. The elevation allows gravity to reduce the flow of blood to your legs, diminishing inflammation.
- Rest helps speed healing of a knee injury. Taking your weight off your knee and minimizing the continual strain allows the injury to heal and avoids any further damage.
- To reduce the inflammation and lessen the pain of a knee injury, take aspirin, ibuprofen, or naproxen. Taking acetaminophen will help relieve the pain, but it won't reduce the swelling, which is the cause of the pain.
- Prevent future knee injuries by doing exercises that strengthen your quadriceps and hamstrings, the muscles that support your knees.

AN UPLIFTING STORY

In 1913, 21-year-old socialite Mary Phelps Jacob, fed up with wearing a clumsy and constricting corsetlike contraption under her ballroom gowns, summoned her personal maid and refused to wear the cumbersome undergarment. "Bring me two of my pocket handkerchiefs," she recalled saying, "and some pink ribbon.... And bring the needle and thread and some pins." Jacob wore her homemade undergarment to a dance, and afterward, her girlfriends insisted on knowing how she had moved about so freely, begging Jacob to make copies of her newly devised bra for them to wear. In 1914, Jacob secured a patent for "the backless brassiere," set up a factory, and went into business manufacturing bras.

How to Soothe Excruciating Toothache Pain with Tabasco Sauce

WHAT YOU NEED
- Tabasco Pepper Sauce
- Cotton swab
- Cotton ball or tampon (optional)

WHAT TO DO

1. Use your finger to apply a dab of Tabasco Pepper Sauce directly to the gum, or use a cotton swab to apply five or six drops directly to a cavity in the tooth. You can also saturate a cotton ball or tampon with the pepper sauce and press it against the affected spot.

2. If your toothache lasts longer than a day or two, if you experience severe pain, or if your toothache is accompanied by fever or earache, see a dentist.

HOW IT WORKS

Applying Tabasco Pepper Sauce to the tender area anesthetizes the pain. Tabasco Pepper Sauce contains the alkaloid capsaicin, a spicy compound proven to numb pain when applied topically. Capsaicin enters nerves and temporarily depletes them of the neurotransmitter that sends pain signals to the brain.

A KICK IN THE TEETH

- A toothache can be caused by a myriad of problems, including tooth decay, a crack or fissure, a piece of food trapped between two teeth, a gum infection, or an abscessed tooth.
- Temporarily reglue a loose crown by putting a dab of toothpaste inside the crown and pressing it back in place. Or cement it back in place with superglue.
- Rinsing your mouth vigorously with lukewarm water several times a day can help dislodge any trapped food debris from your teeth, alleviating toothache pain.
- In 1578, England's Queen Elizabeth endured several weeks of excruciating toothache pain until the bishop of London persuaded her to have the offending tooth pulled—by voluntarily having one of his good teeth extracted to show her that the pain was bearable.

- To avoid exacerbating toothache pain or making the situation worse, refrain from poking at it with a toothpick or your tongue.
- In the 2000 movie *Cast Away*, Chuck Noland (Tom Hanks), stranded on a deserted island in the South Pacific, cures a toothache by knocking out his tooth with the blade of an ice skate.

EVERY TRICK IN THE BOOK
More Toothache Remedies

- **Frozen Peas.** To numb the nerves causing toothache pain until you can see a dentist, cover a bag of frozen peas with a sheet of paper towel and press it against your cheek, over the painful tooth, for 15 minutes every hour. The frozen peas act like small ice cubes, and the bag of peas conforms to the shape of your neck. The paper towel creates a layer of insulation to prevent frostbite.
- **Hydrogen Peroxide.** To temporarily relieve the pain of a toothache, rinse your mouth with hydrogen peroxide. The solution helps kill bacteria that might be exacerbating the pain.
- **Ice Cube.** To help relieve a toothache, cover an ice cube with a thin cloth and rub it on the back of your hand (belonging to the same side of the body as the toothache pain) on the muscle beneath the web of flesh between the thumb and index finger for 5 to 10 minutes.
- **Peanut Butter and Mustard Powder.** To anesthetize toothache pain, place a dollop of peanut butter on the tip of your index finger, sprinkle with mustard powder on it, and stick the glob with the mustard side down on the affected tooth. The peanut butter holds the mustard in place, and the mustard numbs the nerve's endings.
- **Salt.** To quell toothache pain, dissolve 1 teaspoon of salt in a cup of boiled water, let it cool, swish the simple mouthwash around your mouth for 30 seconds, and then spit it out. The saltwater rinses out debris and helps reduce inflammation.
- **Tea Bag.** To soothe a toothache, dampen a tea bag with warm water and press it against the affected tooth. The tannic acid in the tea is an astringent that helps reduce inflammation.
- **Vanilla Extract.** Saturate a cotton ball with vanilla extract and press it against the gum. The high alcohol content of vanilla extract numbs the pain.

How to Immobilize Broken Bones with a Pizza Box and Bubble Wrap

WHAT YOU NEED
- Clean, empty pizza box
- Bubble Wrap
- Duct tape

WHAT TO DO

1. Unfold the pizza box into a flat sheet of corrugated cardboard.
2. Fold the cardboard into the shape of a lengthy triangular or rectangular tube, with sides wide enough to snugly fit the broken appendage.
3. Pad the inside of the center side of the tube with several sheets of Bubble Wrap to create a padded bottom support for the limb. The bubble cushioning also provides comfort and stability.
4. Gently place the affected arm or leg on the padded side of the splint. If the break involves a joint, secure the splint above and below the joint.
5. Place sheets of Bubble Wrap around the rest of the limb.
6. Fold the other cardboard sides of the splint around the appendage.
7. Secure the cardboard splint in place with duct tape, making the splint tight enough to prevent the bone from shifting without cutting off any circulation should the injured limb swell.

HOW IT WORKS
The cardboard splint immobilizes the fractured or dislocated limb to prevent further injury during any subsequent movement—such as getting the victim proper medical attention.

BAD TO THE BONE
- Once the broken limb has been set in a cast, you can avoid damaging the cast by wrapping it with Bubble Wrap (bubble side in, to resist the temptation to pop the bubbles) held in place with duct tape or clear packaging tape.

- You can also improvise a splint from rolled-up newspaper, rolled-up magazines, a broomstick, a ski pole, a ruler, or even a toothbrush (for a broken finger).
- Immobilizing a suspected fracture prevents a broken bone from causing more damage by piercing arteries, severing nerves, or injuring internal organs.
- A splint can be secured in place with torn strips of cloth, belts, neckties, handkerchiefs, bandanas, or rope.
- To immobilize a potentially broken ankle or foot, remove the individual's shoes and socks, tie a pillow around the affected area, and keep the leg elevated.
- To set a simple fracture in an emergency situation, pull in the opposite direction on both sides of the break, realigning the limb in a normal resting position. If the bone is protruding from the skin, do not attempt to set this compound fracture. Instead, stop any bleeding and immobilize the limb with a splint.
- Numbness, tingling, swelling, or excess discoloration in the affected limb indicate a lack of circulation, meaning you should set the bone.

How to Fashion a Sling from Panty Hose

WHAT YOU NEED

- Pair of panty hose
- Scissors (optional)

WHAT TO DO

1. If you break an arm or collarbone, knot the feet of the panty hose together.
2. Place the loop over your head, with the knot behind your neck.
3. Slip your arm into through the crotch area of the panty hose and insert it into one of the legs to create the sling.

4. Adjust the knot to raise or lower the crotch area to make the harness more effective.
5. To make the sling more fashionable, use the scissors to snip off the excess panty hose legs beyond the knot.

HOW IT WORKS

The nylon harness is strong enough to support the weight of your arm, stabilize the injury, and decrease the pain until you can get to a doctor.

NO BONES ABOUT IT

- To make a sling from a sheet of fabric (approximately 3-feet square), fold the cloth in half diagonally to create a triangle. Drape the triangle over your injured forearm as if folding it in half with the corner of the triangle at your elbow. Bring one end of the bandage over the right shoulder, and bring the other end of the bandage over your left shoulder, cradling the arm in the fold. Tie the ends in a knot behind the neck.

How to Treat a Bee or Wasp Sting with a Credit Card and Meat Tenderizer

WHAT YOU NEED

- Credit card
- Meat tenderizer

WHAT TO DO

1. If you're stung by a bee, it will likely leave behind its stinger and attached venom sac. Remove them by lightly scraping the skin with the edge of a credit card to flick it away.
2. For both bee and wasp stings, make a paste of meat tenderizer and water and immediately apply the paste to the sting.
3. Keep the paste on for up to 30 minutes.

HOW IT WORKS

When a bee injects its stinger into flesh, muscles still active in the stinger burrow it deeper into the wound, while other muscles continue pumping venom into your body. Removing the stinger from the skin prevents this from happening. The enzyme papain in meat tenderizer breaks down the proteins in the venom, relieving the stinging sensation and reducing inflammation.

BUZZ OFF

- Bees have stingers for self-defense. Wasps (including hornets and yellow jackets) use their stingers to hunt insects, spiders, and caterpillars to feed their larva. The stinger of a worker honeybee usually detaches when the insect attacks, and the honeybee dies a few hours later. A bumblebee or wasp retains its stinger, enabling it to sting repeatedly.
- Insect venom can trigger an allergic reaction, the severity of which depends on the individual's sensitivity.
- Bees pollinate fruit trees, vegetable plants, and flowers. One simple way to get rid of an abundance of bees is to call a local beekeeper.
- If the area around the bug bite or sting swells larger than 4 inches in diameter, or if you experience nausea, cramps, or diarrhea, see a doctor immediately. If a bug bite or sting triggers difficulty breathing, swelling of the lips or throat, dizziness, vomiting, hives, or rapid heartbeat, call 911 for emergency medical assistance.

EVERY TRICK IN THE BOOK

More Ways to Take the Sting Out

- **Apple Cider Vinegar.** After removing the stinger, saturate a cotton ball with apple cider vinegar and press it against the sting for 5 minutes. The acetic acid neutralizes the venom, soothes the pain, and reduces the inflammation.
- **Baking Soda.** To stop a bee or wasp sting from burning, mix 1 tablespoon of baking soda with enough water to make a thick paste and cover the affected area with the paste. The alkaline sodium bicarbonate neutralizes acidic bee or wasp venom.
- **Sugar.** Mix 1 teaspoon of sugar in enough water to make a thick paste and apply it to the insect sting. The sugar neutralizes the poison from the sting.
- **Tea Bags.** To sterilize and soothe a bee or wasp sting, dampen a tea bag with warm water and press it against the sting. The tannin in the tea acts as an astringent, tightening the skin, reducing inflammation and irritation and drawing infection from the skin.
- **Toothpaste.** To relieve bee, wasp, or hornet stings, rub a dab of toothpaste into the affected area. No one knows why it works, although some people suspect the menthol in the mint, while others suspect the glycerol.

How to Kill Head Lice with Mayonnaise

WHAT YOU NEED
- Jar of mayonnaise
- Plastic wrap (or shower cap)
- Towel
- Plastic trash bags
- Shampoo
- White vinegar
- Nit comb

WHAT TO DO
1. Saturate the hair completely with mayonnaise. Be sure to work the mayonnaise in the hair and roots well. The hair must be extremely greasy from the mayonnaise to prevent lice from breathing.
2. Wrap the hair as tightly as possible with plastic wrap (or a shower cap) and then wrap the plastic wrap with a towel.
3. Allow the mayonnaise to remain on the head for 2 hours to kill all the lice. During this time take all pillowcases, towels, blankets, sheets, and clothes that have come into contact with any lice-infested hair and run them through the washing machine and dryer.
4. Place all comforters, quilts, and stuffed animals in plastic trash bags, tie the bags shut, and store them in the garage for two weeks. Lice cannot survive without a human host. The eggs take one week to hatch, so after two weeks all the lice will be dead.
5. Shampoo the hair thoroughly. Rinse the hair with white vinegar and then rinse it clean with water.
6. Comb hair with a nit comb.
7. Repeat the treatment in 7 days if desired.

HOW IT WORKS
The oils in the mayonnaise suffocate head lice and also condition hair. Adult lice lay eggs, called nits, which stick like glue to the hair shafts. The vinegar dissolves the "glue," allowing you to comb the nits from hair easily with a nit comb.

HEADS UP

- Most people resort to a lice shampoo containing the pesticide pyrethrin (derived from chrysanthemums) or permethrin (a synthetic form of pyrethrin). Recent studies indicate that lice are becoming pyrethrin resistant.
- Lice burrow into the scalp to feed on human blood. A chemical in their saliva stops blood from clotting. The chemical causes the incessant itching.
- Female lice lay up to 10 eggs a day.
- Lice die within 12 to 24 hours without a human head to feed on, and, contrary to popular belief, they cannot jump, nor will they transfer to your pets.
- The word *louse*, the singular form of the word *lice*, is slang for "a bad person."
- The word *nitwit* originated from the false idea that head lice infest only poor, uneducated children.
- The term *nit-picking* originated from the tedious act of having to pick every nit from the head of a person infested with lice.
- The expression "going over it with a fine-tooth comb" stems from combing the hair of a lice-infested person with a fine-tooth comb to get rid of all the nits.

How to Treat Poison Ivy with Nail Polish Remover

WHAT YOU NEED
- Soap and water
- Cotton balls
- Nail polish remover (containing acetone)

WHAT TO DO
1. Within 15 minutes of contact with poison ivy, wash the contaminated skin with soap and water.
2. Immediately afterward, use a cotton ball to apply nail polish remover to the area. Use a fresh cotton ball every time you touch it with the bottle of nail polish remover, to avoid contaminating the bottle. Carefully discard the used cotton balls.
3. Wash the affected area of skin with soap and water to remove the nail polish remover from your skin.
4. Carefully remove your clothes and launder them in the washing machine with hot water and your regular detergent. Urushiol oil, the active ingredient in poison ivy, adheres to clothes and shoes, and any skin that comes into contact with it can break out in a rash.

HOW IT WORKS
According to the *New York Times*, the acetone in the nail polish remover will remove some of the urushiol, the oil in poison ivy that rapidly penetrates the skin and combines with skin proteins to trigger an allergic reaction, thus reducing the severity of the itching and possibly preventing a rash altogether.

DON'T BE RASH
- The active ingredient in poison ivy and poison oak is urushiol oil, one of the most potent external toxins known to humans. The average person breaks out in a rash after coming into contact with just one ten-millionth of a gram of urushiol oil.
- Once you come into contact with poison ivy, poison oak, or poison sumac, you have 15 minutes to wash off the urushiol—the sticky oil that adheres to your skin—before your body launches an allergic reaction.

- To avoid contact with poison plants, abide by the adage "Leaves of three, let it be."
- The blistery rash from poison ivy, appearing anywhere from 2 hours to two weeks after contact with urushiol, generally lasts three weeks but can linger for up to eight weeks.
- A poison ivy, poison oak, or poison sumac rash is not contagious, nor can the fluid from a blister spread the rash.
- Inhaling smoke from burning poison ivy, poison oak, or poison sumac can irritate or injure your eyes or nasal passages. The smoke contains the urushiol oil.
- Although dogs and cats are immune to urushiol, their coats can get covered with the oil, which can then come into contact with you or others.
- To avoid getting poison ivy, poison oak, or poison sumac, learn how to recognize these poison plants before venturing into the wild, and if necessary wear long pants and a long sleeved shirt.
- If the rash covers a large area of your body and feels excruciating, or if the rash affects your eyes, mouth, or private parts, consult a doctor. Also seek medication attention if the blisters ooze (to prevent infection) or the rash lasts longer than three weeks.

How to Remove Cactus Spines with Elmer's Glue

WHAT YOU NEED

- White glue
- Antibiotic ointment
- Adhesive bandages

WHAT TO DO

1. Attempting to remove a cactus spine from your skin can inadvertently drive the spine deeper into the skin. Instead, pour a dollop of white glue (approximately the size of a nickel) over each embedded spine, making sure to coat the part of the needle protruding from the skin.
2. Let the glue dry undisturbed. This should take up to 30 minutes.
3. To remove the cactus spine, peel the dried glue off the skin, in the opposite direction from how the spine went into the skin.
4. Wash the affected area with antibacterial soap, dry thoroughly, and apply antibiotic ointment and an adhesive bandage to prevent infection.

HOW IT WORKS

The dried glue adheres to the cactus spine, so when you peel off the glue, the cactus spine comes out with it.

STUCK ON YOU

- Using glue to remove a cactus spine from skin is similar to using hot wax to remove unwanted body hair. Hair-removing wax cloths or body wax can also be used to remove cactus spines as well.
- You can also remove cactus spines from skin with a strip of duct tape, but stripping the duct tape from the skin is more painful than peeling off dried glue.
- To remove thin, hairlike cactus spines from the skin, put on a pair of rubber gloves and brush the affected area with a balled-up pair of clean, used panty hose in the opposite direction that the cactus spine went into the skin. The panty hose removes the needles, which adhere to the nylon hose. Discard the panty hose and gloves.
- Soaking the affected area with warm water for 10 to 15 minutes engorges the spine and softens the skin, making the thorn easier to remove with tweezers.
- To remove small cactus needles, rubbing a sheet of paper towel saturated with baby oil across the affected area removes most of the needles.

How to Soothe Severe Sunburn Pain with Iced Tea Mix

WHAT YOU NEED
- Jar of powdered ice tea mix
- Bathtub
- Water

WHAT TO DO
1. Empty a jar of powdered ice tea mix into a bathtub.
2. Fill the bathtub with cool water.
3. Stir the bathwater with your hand to dissolve the powdered tea mix.
4. Soak in the tea for 10 to 15 minutes.

HOW IT WORKS
The tannin in the tea relieves sunburn pain.

EVERYTHING UNDER THE SUN
- To prevent sunburn, apply sunscreen with a sun protection factor (SPF) of 30 or higher to your skin at least 30 minutes before going outdoors, and limit the amount of time you spend in the sun. Reapply sunscreen every 2 hours.
- To protect your body from sunburn, wear long pants, a long-sleeve shirt, sunglasses, and a wide-brimmed hat.
- Stay out of the sun between 10 AM and 4 PM, when the sun's rays are strongest.
- After swimming or perspiring heavily, reapply sunscreen.
- You can get a sunburn on cloudy, overcast days—the sun's ultraviolet rays penetrate clouds—and in the winter from sunshine reflected off snow and ice.
- Sunburned skin heals itself within a few days (or longer, depending on the severity of the burn). The top layer of damaged skin peels off. The new layer of skin usually appears discolored for a short time.
- Sunburn can affect any part of your body, including your scalp, lips, ears, and eyes.
- You can relieve the pain and inflammation of sunburn by dampening a washcloth with ice-cold water and applying it to the affected area as a compress for 10 minutes several times a day.

- To prevent dehydration and offset the desiccating effects of sunburn on the skin, drink plenty of water or juice to replenish those lost fluids.
- If your sunburn blisters, if you experience chills or a fever, or if the pain becomes excruciating, consult your doctor. If nausea, vomiting, headache, or fainting accompanies the sunburn, seek immediate medical attention to rule out heat exhaustion or heatstroke.

EVERY TRICK IN THE BOOK
More Ways to Take the Heat Off

Here are a few more simple ways to relieve sunburn pain.

- **Baking Soda.** Mix one handful of baking soda in a bathtub filled with cool water and soak for 20 minutes. The sodium bicarbonate soothes inflammation, and the cool water relieves the pain.
- **Mustard.** For instant relief from sunburn pain, slather yellow mustard on the burn to stop the stinging and prevent blistering. Let the mustard dry on the skin.
- **Quaker Oats.** To relieve sunburn pain, cut one foot from a clean, used pair of panty hose, then grind 1 cup of uncooked Quaker Oats in a blender and pour the fine powder into the foot. Tie a knot in the open end and tie this to the bathtub faucet. Fill the bathtub with cool water, soak for 15 minutes or more, and let your body air-dry so the soothing oats stay on your skin.
- **Toothpaste.** To soothe sunburn, apply toothpaste as an ointment to the affected area. The glycerin in the toothpaste provides a soothing, cooling sensation and fast, temporary relief.
- **Vinegar.** Saturate a few sheets of paper towel with white vinegar and wrap them around the sunburned skin (avoiding the eyes). Let the paper towels sit until the vinegar dries. The acetic acid in the vinegar helps relieve the pain and inflammation.
- **Yogurt.** To relieve sunburn pain, smear yogurt over the affected area.

How to Treat Hypothermia with Aluminum Foil

WHAT YOU NEED
- Hat
- Scarf (or cloth)
- Towel
- Aluminum foil
- Blanket

WHAT TO DO

1. If a person's body temperature drops below 95°F, cover the person's head with a hat and wrap the neck with a scarf (or cloth) to slow the loss of heat from the head.
2. Move the victim inside a warm, dry shelter.
3. Remove any wet clothes from the person and pat the skin dry with a towel.
4. If the individual is conscious, have him or her dress in dry clothes.
5. Wrap the clothed person in aluminum foil, with the shiny side facing the body. For greater effectiveness, wrap the person in a blanket and then wrap the aluminum foil around the blanket.
6. Also wrap aluminum foil (shiny side in) around the victim's socks or shoes.
7. If you wish to have the victim lie down, place a layer of aluminum foil under a blanket or sleeping bag and have the victim lie on top of that. This helps reflect body heat to keep the victim warmer.

HOW IT WORKS

Excessive body heat loss leads to hypothermia, but wrapping the body in aluminum foil reflects body heat back to the body and stops both evaporative and convective heat loss.

When a person perspires in cold weather, the perspiration evaporates, making the body colder. The aluminum foil helps slow the process of evaporative heat loss by increasing the humidity of the air next to the skin. In convective heat loss, cold wind takes the warmth away from the body. Wearing a layer of aluminum foil as insulation reduces convective heat loss by providing insulation.

FREEZING YOUR TAIL OFF

- Hypothermia occurs when the body temperature drops to below 95°F.
- When the body temperature drops, the body begins to shiver to produce body heat. If the body gets colder, the shivering ceases.
- Hypothermia can lead to loss of consciousness. If the victim is left untreated, breathing slows, the heart stops pumping blood, and death results.
- Falling through the ice of a frozen lake or river, taking a plunge into cold water, or getting soaking wet in a rainstorm could cause hypothermia.
- To avoid hypothermia, get out of the risky environment, change into dry clothes, wrap yourself in a space blanket, and sit by a warm fireplace or heater. Drink warm water sweetened with sugar, which quickly gives the body a source of energy to help warm the core. Aerobic activity—such as running in place or doing jumping jacks—also helps generate warmth.
- To help prevent hypothermia, trace each foot on a piece of aluminum foil and add a ½-inch border. Place the foil insoles inside your shoes, sneakers, or boots with the shiny side up. The radiant heat from your feet will add extra warmth to your footwear.

How to Remove Broken Glass from Skin with Duct Tape

WHAT YOU NEED

- Epsom salt (optional)
- Basin (optional)
- Water (optional)
- Washcloth (optional)
- Duct tape

WHAT TO DO

1. If possible, dissolve 2 tablespoons of Epsom salt in a basin filled with warm water and soak the affected area in the solution for 10 minutes. Or saturate a washcloth with the solution and apply the washcloth to the area for 10 minutes. The briny solution swells the skin, draws the shard out of the skin, and soothes the pain, making the shard of glass easier to remove.
2. Adhere a strip of duct tape to the area where the shard of glass is embedded in the skin.
3. Let the tape remain on the skin for a several minutes.
4. Gently press the tape against the shard of glass to ensure adhesion.
5. Gently peel off the tape in the opposite direction that the glass shard went into the skin.
6. If other shards of glass remain embedded in the skin, repeat the process.

HOW IT WORKS

The strip of duct tape adheres to the shard of glass, so when the duct tape is pulled off, the tape pulls the glass out of the skin.

PEOPLE WHO LIVE IN GLASS HOUSES

- Hair-removing wax cloths or body wax can also be used to remove glass shards from skin.
- To remove a small glass shard from your skin using suction, carefully fill a clean, empty glass beer or soda bottle with boiling water and then empty the water from the bottle. Press the mouth of the bottle over the spot where the glass shard is embedded in the skin and wait for the bottle to cool. The boiling water heats the air in the bottle, causing the

molecules to move far apart from each other. As the air in the bottle cools, the molecules move closer together, causing a partial vacuum and creating suction, drawing the glass shard from the skin. Soaking the affected area in Epsom salt beforehand helps facilitate the extraction.

- If you're unable to remove a shard of glass with tweezers or any of the above methods, seek medical attention to avoid infection or any internal damage to blood vessels, tissue, or nerves.

How to Stitch a Wound with Condoms and Dental Floss

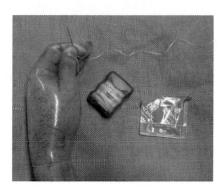

WHAT YOU NEED

- Water
- Vodka, bleach (5.25 percent sodium hypochlorite), or Listerine mouthwash (original formula)
- Sewing needle
- Pair of pliers (ideally needle-nose)
- Matches or butane lighter (optional)
- Dental floss (plain, not mint-flavored)
- 2 condoms
- Scissors (or knife)

WHAT TO DO

1. A deep laceration requires stitches and medical attention, but if you find yourself in a remote part of the world and butterfly bandages are unavailable or do not work, you may need to suture the wound.
2. Elevate the injured area above the heart.
3. Before stitching the wound, clean it thoroughly to prevent infection. Wash the wound with bottled water, remove any foreign objects from the wound, and wash with water a second time.
4. Disinfect the wound by saturating it with vodka, diluted bleach (3 ounces bleach to 4 cups water), or Listerine mouthwash (original formula).
5. Using the pliers, bend the needle to create a crescent shape.
6. Sterilize the needle and pliers with a flame, vodka, diluted bleach, or Listerine.
7. Thread the dental floss through the eye of the needle.
8. To improvise surgical gloves, wear condoms on your hands or around several fingers.
9. Pinch the wound together, insert the needle through the skin on one side of the midpoint of the laceration (⅛ inch from the edge of the gash), through the bottom of the wound, and back out on the other side of the skin. If necessary, use the pliers to push and pull the

needle through the skin. (Sewing through the bottom of the wound enables the floss to grip equal quantities of tissue on both sides of the laceration to align the edges of skin. This technique also prevents the formation of air and blood pockets.)

10. Gently pull the ends of the floss, to pull the center of the two sides of the wound together, and tie a double knot—just tightly enough to seal the wound without killing the tissue.

11. Using the scissors, clip off the excess dental floss.

12. Sew a second suture halfway between one end of the laceration and the middle stitch.

13. Sew a third suture halfway between the opposite end of the laceration and the middle stitch.

14. Repeat the process of sewing sutures halfway between existing stitches until you have effectually sealed the wound.

15. Keep the stitches dry to prevent water from getting into the wound, increasing the risk of infection, and potentially opening the wound after the stitches are removed.

16. Seek medical attention as soon as possible. If medical attention is unavailable, remove the stitches after 5 days for a face gash, 7 days for a laceration on the body, and 10 to 14 days for a gash on the foot.

HOW IT WORKS

Stitching a wound holds the two sides of the lacerated skin as close to original condition as possible so the two sides can heal together.

A STITCH IN TIME

- Dakin's solution, developed during World War I by English chemist Henry Drysdale Dakin and French surgeon Alexis Carrel, kills germs and prevents germ growth in wounds. To make the solution, boil 4 cups of water for 15 minutes, remove from heat, add ½ teaspoon of baking soda, and then add 3 ounces of bleach (5.25 percent sodium hypochlorite).

- A sutured wound requires approximately 72 hours for the stitched skin to close and become airtight.

- The best way to close a deep laceration is to disinfect the wound, line up the edges of the laceration, and, starting at the midpoint of the wound, apply a sterile adhesive butterfly bandage across the skin as you push the edges of the skin together. Apply these bandages along the length of the laceration.

7

DISASTER RELIEF

Flash floods threaten your home. The temperature drops and you lose all power. A skunk sprays your dog, and mice infest the house. Is all lost? Not if you've got trash bags, aluminum foil, a disposable douche, and fabric softener—and the chutzpah to use them in unorthodox ways.

How to Make Flood Boots with Trash Bags

WHAT YOU NEED
- 2 plastic trash bags
- Duct tape (optional)

WHAT TO DO
1. Wearing sneakers or shoes, insert each foot inside a plastic trash bag.
2. Pull the plastic tie cord snugly to seal the trash bag around your upper calves or above your knees.
3. Tie the plastic tie cord with a double shoelace knot.
4. To secure the plastic bag in place, tape the top edge of the bag to the legs of your pants with strips of duct tape adhered vertically. Then wrap strips of duct tape around your pants leg and the top of the bag.

HOW IT WORKS
The waterproof plastic bags turn your typical shoes or sneakers into emergency snow boots or flood boots.

COME HELL OR HIGH WATER
- Trash bags make excellent waterproof boots when water from the toilet, washing machine, or bathtub accidentally floods the floor.
- Trash bag boots are also ideal for working in poison ivy. When you're finished working, turn the bags inside out and dispose of them.
- A small plastic trash bag can also be used to waterproof a cast. Simply slip the cast inside the bag and seal the top shut with tape or a rubber band.

How to Build a Dike with Trash Bags

WHAT YOU NEED

- Plastic trash bags
- Shovel
- Sand or dirt
- Duct tape

WHAT TO DO

1. Double-bag two plastic trash bags by placing one bag inside the other.
2. Open a trash bag and place it on the ground with the inside bottom visible. Or have another person hold the trash bag open for you.
3. Shovel a scoop of sand or dirt inside the bag and then hold up the edges of the bag and shovel more sand or dirt into the mouth of the bag until the bag is halfway full.

4. Pull the plastic drawstring tight, flatten the bag to remove any trapped air, and tie a knot in the drawstring.
5. Wrap the excess plastic around the sand-filled half of the bag and secure it in place with duct tape.
6. Wrap duct tape around the shortest width of the bag in two or three locations.
7. Repeat the procedure to create as many sandbags as you need to build an effective dike.
8. If floodwaters threaten to inundate your home, stack the plastic sandbags as if you were laying bricks to build a wall to divert the water away from your house. Be sure to build the dike in your yard on the side of your house toward which water will be flowing. **Never build a dike directly against a wall**; the weight of the sandbags can weaken the structure.
9. Build the dike with a bottom thickness two or three times the finished height. (For instance, a dike 3 feet tall should have a bottom 6 to 9 feet thick.)

10. If you intend to build the dike more than 3 feet tall, dig a trench 6 inches deep and 2 feet across in which to stack the bottom row of bags. Doing so stabilizes the embankment.

HOW IT WORKS

Filling a trash bag halfway full of sand or dirt turns the plastic bag into a sandbag. Wrapping the bag with duct tape strengthens the bag and provides traction to help hold the bags in place.

WATER OVER THE DAM

- Filling a 16-gallon trash bag halfway full of sand or dirt turns the plastic bag into a 40-pound sandbag.
- In a pinch, you can fill sandbags with small gravel.
- If need be, fashion sandbags from pillowcases, tied-off T-shirts and pants, socks, and ziplock storage bags.

How to Boost a Cast-Iron Radiator with Aluminum Foil

WHAT YOU NEED

- Ruler
- Pencil
- Sheet of corrugated cardboard
- Scissors
- Heavy-duty aluminum foil
- Tape or glue

WHAT TO DO

1. Using a ruler and pencil, measure a sheet of corrugated cardboard to the height and width of your cast-iron radiator.
2. Using scissors, cut out the measured rectangle of the cardboard.
3. Tape or glue heavy-duty aluminum foil to the cardboard, with the shiny side of the foil facing out.
4. Place the sheet of cardboard behind your cast-iron radiator with the shiny side facing the radiator. Make sure the aluminum foil does not touch the radiator; otherwise, the aluminum foil will start conducting heat, rather than reflecting it.
5. If the radiator has a cover, tape aluminum foil under the cover's top (again with the shiny side facing the radiator).

HOW IT WORKS

The foil-covered heat reflector reflects the radiant heat waves generated by the radiator back into the room instead of into the wall behind the radiator. The reflector also helps prevent convection currents from being transmitted through the wall by way of conduction.

WARM AS TOAST

- If you don't have any aluminum foil, you can use a space blanket to create a radiator reflector.
- If you don't have any corrugated cardboard, you can tape the aluminum foil to the wall behind the radiator.
- Aluminum foil can also be used to speed up your ironing and conserve energy. Cover the ironing board with aluminum foil, with the shiny side up, and then put the ironing cover over it. The foil reflects the heat back up as you iron, heating the backside of the fabric you're ironing.

How to Repair Broken Eyeglasses with Dental Floss

WHAT YOU NEED
- Dental floss
- Scissors

WHAT TO DO

1. If the screw from the hinge of your eyeglasses falls out and gets lost, line up the hinge and thread a piece of dental floss through the screw holes.
2. Tie a double knot in the dental floss.
3. Use scissors to trim off the excess dental floss.

4. Buy a replacement screw (or eyeglass repair kit) to fix the hinge properly. Or take the glasses to an eyewear shop for repair.

HOW IT WORKS

The strong, durable waxed floss holds the hinge in place unobtrusively.

FOR YOUR EYES ONLY

- **Adhesive Bandage.** If your eyeglasses break, use an adhesive bandage to tape them back together temporarily.
- **Chewing Gum.** If a lens in your eyeglasses is loose, use a small piece of chewing gum (well-chewed so all the sugar is gone) in the corner of the lens to hold it in place. In a pinch, you can also use a well-chewed piece of gum to reattach a pair of eyeglasses broken at the nose bridge.
- **Clear Nail Polish.** To prevent the screws in eyeglasses from loosening, apply a small drop of clear nail polish to the threads of the screws before tightening them.
- **Paper Clip.** Insert a paper clip into the screw hole to secure the frames.
- **Safety Pin.** A small safety pin can be used to hold the hinge together, but *be careful that the safety pin doesn't accidentally open* and prick you in the face or eye.
- **Twist Tie.** Strip the paper from a twist tie, and thread the thin metal wire through the screw hole and twist the ends together to hold the hinge together. Be sure to *wrap the ends of the wire around the frame* to prevent them from scratching your face.

How to Make Homemade Laundry Soap with Borax

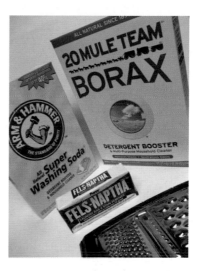

WHAT YOU NEED

- Knife
- Bar of Fels-Naptha soap
- Ziplock storage bag
- Grater
- Measuring cup
- Water
- Saucepan
- Wooden spoon
- Bucket
- 2 tablespoons of borax
- 4 tablespoons of Arm & Hammer Super Washing Soda (not baking soda)
- Plastic wrap
- 2 clean, empty 1-gallon plastic water jugs

WHAT TO DO

1. Using a knife, cut the bar of Fels-Naptha soap into fourths and store three of the quarters in a ziplock storage bag (for next time).
2. Grate one quarter of the Fels-Naptha soap.
3. Place the shredded soap and 1 cup of water in a saucepan. Cook over medium-low heat, stirring constantly with a wooden spoon until the soap dissolves.

4. Pour 10 cups of water into the bucket. Add the dissolved soap mixture, borax, and washing soda. Stir well, add 10 more cups of water, and stir thoroughly.
5. Cover the bucket with a sheet of plastic wrap and let it sit overnight.
6. In the morning, stir the gelled soap mixture, add 20 cups of water, and stir well.
7. Pour the soap into two 1-gallon plastic water jugs and seal closed. Shake well before using.
8. Use ⅝ cup of the homemade soap per load in a regular washer. Use ¼ cup per load in a high-efficiency washer.

HOW IT WORKS

The combination of Fels-Naptha soap, borax, and washing soda makes an inexpensive and potent laundry soap.

IT ALL COMES OUT IN THE WASH

- In 1893, Fels & Company, founded by Lazarus Fels three decades earlier, began making Fels-Naptha soap, which came to be used for washing laundry by hand.
- Borax, a naturally occurring mineral, whitens clothes, aids in the removal of stains and soil, and deodorizes clothes.
- Washing soda is sodium carbonate, which softens water and helps remove grease.
- If you wish to experiment with homemade laundry soap, you can add baking soda to help dissolve dirt and grease, OxiClean to help remove stains, and a few drops of your favorite essential oil to give the soap an appealing scent.

How to Find a Lost Contact Lens with Panty Hose

WHAT YOU NEED
- Panty hose
- Scissors
- Vacuum cleaner with hose attachment
- Rubber bands

WHAT TO DO

1. If you lose a contact lens, an earring back, a rhinestone, or any small item in the carpeting, cut off the foot from a clean, used pair of panty hose with a pair of scissors.
2. Slip the end of the vacuum cleaner hose into the panty hose foot, pull the nylon so it is taut over the hose opening, and secure it in place with a few rubber bands.
3. Vacuum an inch above the carpet where you suspect you dropped the object, frequently checking the panty hose to see if you've sucked up the contact lens or other object.
4. Be sure to rinse the contact lens well and sterilize it in cleaning solution before placing it in your eye.

HOW IT WORKS

The suction from the vacuum cleaner sucks up the lightweight contact lens, but the panty hose creates a filter to catch the lens and prevent it from getting sucked into the machine.

LOOKING HIGH AND LOW

- Don't have a vacuum cleaner? A cordless DustBuster works equally well.
- If you don't have any rubber bands, use a pair of scissors to cut a 1-inch-thick cuff from the sleeve of a rubber glove, creating a giant rubber band.
- If you accidentally drop a contact lens, earring, or ring down a bathroom sink drain, attach a piece of nylon hose over the end of a wet/dry shop vacuum hose. Remove the drain stopper, position the end of the hose over the drain, and turn on the vacuum. The powerful shop vac sucks up the water and contact lens, trapping the lens in the nylon net.

How to Get Rid of Mice and Rats with Fabric Softener

WHAT YOU NEED
- Box of Bounce Outdoor Fresh dryer sheets
- Binder clips (or clothespins)
- Spray bottle
- Water

WHAT TO DO
1. To stop mice or rats from entering your home, place individual dryer sheets in crevices, small cracks, holes, or wherever you wish to repel them. You can also shove the dryer sheets into the tailpipe of a car, truck, or recreational vehicle to keep mice or rats from infesting the vehicle.
2. Secure the dryer sheets in place with the binder clips.
3. To refresh the dryer sheets, fill a spray bottle with water and mist the dryer sheets once a week or whenever they seem to stop exuding the familiar oleander scent. The water revitalizes the fragrance.

HOW IT WORKS
The fragrance infused in sheets of original, classic Bounce (now packaged as Outdoor Fresh) is oleander, which naturally repels rodents.

PLAYING CAT AND MOUSE
- Procter & Gamble currently manufactures eight varieties of Bounce: Outdoor Fresh, Fresh Linen, Spring Fresh, Meadows & Rain, Spring & Renewal, Fresh Lavender, and Bounce Free. Only Outdoor Fresh contains oleander. In other words, the other varieties will not repel rodents.
- If you want to catch mice or rats in traditional traps, do not bait the traps with cheese. Mice and rats can remove the cheese without setting off the trap. Instead, bait the traps with peanut butter, which is almost impossible to remove from a trap without springing it.
- To prevent mice and rats from squeezing through small cracks and holes in wallboards, plug the openings with steel wool pads.

- Bounce can also be used to repel mosquitoes (by wearing a sheet through a belt loop) and gophers or moles (by shoving a few sheets into the tunnel openings).

How to Repel Mosquitoes with Mouthwash

WHAT YOU NEED
- Listerine (original formula)
- Spray bottle

WHAT TO DO
1. Pour some original formula Listerine into a trigger spray bottle.
2. Spray the "mediciny" mouthwash over your body (avoiding open wounds, which will sting).
3. Also spray a light mist on tables, chairs, screen doors, walls, and floors.
4. Repeat steps 2 and 3 once an hour.

HOW IT WORKS
Listerine repels mosquitoes, possibly with greater effectiveness than DEET. Eucalyptol, the main active ingredient in Listerine, is derived from eucalyptus oil, a common ingredient in botanical insect repellents. Clinical studies show that eucalyptol repels mosquitoes. Listerine also contains thymol and menthol, two essential oils that reputedly repel mosquitoes.

WHAT'S THE BUZZ?
- Applying Listerine to mosquito bites stops the itching.
- You can also repel mosquitoes by slathering Vicks VapoRub on your arms and legs. Mosquitoes hate the smell of Vicks VapoRub. Also, people hate the smell of Vicks VapoRub, which enables you to simultaneously repel in-laws, neighbors, and door-to-door salesmen.
- The Centers for Disease Control and Prevention rates oil of lemon eucalyptus one of the most effective mosquito repellents, along with DEET and picaridin.
- Wearing a pair of clean, used panty hose over your head repels mosquitos and other insects, like gnats. Just be sure to avoid walking into a bank.
- Commercial eucalyptus-based mosquito repellents typically contain up to 75 percent eucalyptus. Listerine contains less than 1 percent eucalyptol.

How to Make a Flyswatter with Duct Tape

WHAT YOU NEED
- Wire clothes hanger
- Duct tape

WHAT TO DO
1. Stretch a wire clothes hanger so that the triangle becomes a long, narrow oval less than 1 inch wide.
2. Bend the hook to form a closed loop.
3. Cut three 10-inch strips of duct tape.
4. Attach the three strips together, sticky side up, by overlapping the sides to form a piece of fabric 5 inches wide by 10 inches long.
5. Place the wire loop formed by the bent hook on the sticky side of a 5-inch side of the duct tape rectangle.
6. Fold the length of the duct tape rectangle in half, enveloping the wire loop and pressing the sticky sides against each other to form the flyswatter pad.

7. Widen the opposite end of the wire oval to form a handle.
8. Wrap duct tape around the handle, ½ inch away from the end, to form an adequate grip.
9. Holding the end of the wire handle, use the homemade fly swatter to swat flies.

HOW IT WORKS
The floppy square of duct tape at the end of the long wire enables you to effectively swat flies from a distance, and the loop of wire at the end of the handle lets you hang the tool from a hook when you're not using it.

WOULDN'T HURT A FLY
- To catch flies with a humane trap, place a small piece of raw meat (or other bait to flies) on a countertop. Lay two pencils parallel to each other on opposite sides of the bait. Rest the mouth of an upside-down jar on the pencils. When a fly steps under the jar, tap on the bottom

of the jar. The fly will instinctively fly upward to escape, getting trapped in the jar. Slide a piece of cardboard under the mouth of the jar, carry the jar outside, and release the insect.

- Mix a teaspoon of dishwashing liquid in a trigger-spray bottle filled with water. Shake well and spray flies. They die instantly. The dishwashing liquid instantly penetrates the insect's exoskeleton.
- To trap flies, pour some molasses in a saucer and set it wherever flies are congregating. The flies, attracted to the sweet molasses, get stuck in it.
- If you're unable to hit flies with a flyswatter, spray the insects with hairspray. The fixative in the hair spray freezes their wings, and the flies fall to the ground, immobilized.

How to Warm Cold Sheets with a Soda Bottle

WHAT YOU NEED

- Clean, empty 1- or 2-liter soda bottle with cap
- Hot water (not boiling)

WHAT TO DO

1. Pour hot water into the soda bottle.
2. Screw the cap on tightly.
3. Ten minutes before you're ready to go to bed, place the bottle between the sheets where you rest your torso.
4. Wait 2 minutes and then move the bottle to where you rest your legs.
5. Wait another 2 minutes and then slowly roll the bottle back and forth from the bottom of the sheets to the pillow.
6. Get into bed with the bottle between your thighs, or lie on your side with the bottle cradled in your arms against your stomach.

HOW IT WORKS

The convective heat from the hot water in the bottle warms the sheets and your body.

POPSICLE TOES

- In the nineteenth century, homes were equipped with ceramic foot warmers—jugs to be filled with hot water and slipped between cold sheets to warm them.
- Europeans and colonial Americans placed a warming pan—a long-handled metal pan filled with hot coals and covered with a lid—between the icy sheets of a bed to warm them.
- After the advent of rubber, the hot-water bottle replaced the warming pan.
- In 1912, American physician Sidney I. Russell invented the first electric blanket. It warmed the bed from *under* the sheets.

How to Avoid Leeches with Panty Hose

WHAT YOU NEED
- Pair of panty hose

WHAT TO DO
1. Before wading through a swamp, put on a pair of panty hose underneath your pants.
2. Tuck the legs of your pants into your boots or socks.
3. Tuck your shirt into your pants.
4. Move quickly and avoid brushing against vegetation.

HOW IT WORKS
The tight weave of the nylon panty hose prevents leeches from attaching to your skin.

SHAKE A LEG
- Leeches attach themselves with anterior suckers and release an anesthetic, which prevents the host from feeling them, and an anticoagulant, which allows the host's blood to flow without clotting. Leeches remain attached until they become engorged, at which point, they drop off to digest the blood.
- Applying alcohol, salt, vinegar, Listerine, a lit cigarette, or a flame will prompt a leech to release its grip and fall off, but these methods can cause the leech to vomit the contents of its stomach into the wound, increasing the risk of infection.
- Attempting to pry the leech off can break off the leech's jaw, leaving parts embedded in the skin. Its jaw parts are left behind.
- In 2003, the *Chicago Tribune* reported that US military personnel in Iraq wore panty hose to protect themselves from sand fleas.
- During the Vietnam War, soldiers wore panty hose to prevent leeches from attaching to their legs when patrolling through marshes.
- When filling a water container in leech-infested waters, cover the mouth of the container with a bandana as a filter to keep leeches out.
- To prevent leeches from crawling up your pant legs, put rubber bands around the cuffs of your pant legs to hold them against your ankles. No rubber bands? Use duct tape or shoe laces or make elastic bands by cutting off 1-inch-wide bands from the cuff of a rubber glove.

Plentiful Purposes for Panty Hose

- **Bandages.** In first aid, you can use a leg cut from a pair of panty hose to fashion a tourniquet, secure a gauze dressing in place, or tie a heating pad or ice pack to a patient.
- **Belt.** In a pinch, a panty hose leg can be used as a substitute for a belt to hold up a pair of pants.
- **Blister Protector.** To prevent blisters, cut off the feet at the ankles from a pair of panty hose and wear them under your socks. The nylon reduces friction between your shoe and your foot.
- **Cord.** Use a panty hose leg as a substitute for twine.
- **Gloves.** To improvise gloves for warmth, cut off the feet from a pair of clean, used panty hose and wear them on your hands. Or better yet, wear a pair of socks on your hands.
- **Insect Net.** To keep gnats, mosquitoes, and black flies from biting your face, ears, head, or neck, wear a clean, used pair of panty hose over your head. The nylon netting keeps bugs at bay. Just be sure to remove the panty hose from your head before walking into a bank or liquor store. You can also wear a pair of panty hose under your pants to protect your legs from chiggers, ticks, and other biting insects.
- **Jellyfish.** Before wading through saltwater, put on a pair of panty hose to protect yourself from jellyfish stings. If you have a second pair of panty hose, cut a hole in the crotch and wear the panty hose over your head like a long-sleeve shirt.
- **Long Underwear.** Wearing a pair of panty hose as an extra layer beneath your clothes provides insulation to keep your body warm in cold weather.
- **Pouch.** Cut off the leg from a pair of panty hose at the knee and use the nylon pouch as a bag to carry small objects.
- **Water Filter.** To strain debris from water collected for drinking, pour the water through the nylon netting of a clean, used pair of panty hose.
- **Window Screen Patch.** To temporarily fix a tear in a window screen or tent screen, cut a patch from a clean, used pair of panty hose. Sew the patch over the hole with needle and thread, or, if need be, dental floss.

How to Get Rid of Skunk Odor with Disposable Douche

WHAT YOU NEED
- Massengill Disposable Douche
- Bucket
- Water
- Sponge

WHAT TO DO
1. Mix two packets of Massengill Disposable Douche in a bucket with water, following the directions on the package.
2. Use a sponge to wash yourself or your sprayed animal with the feminine hygiene product.
3. Let soak for 15 minutes.
4. Rinse clean with water.
5. Bathe your pet with shampoo and rinse well. For humans, simply wash the douche off your body with soap and water.
6. Repeat if necessary.

HOW IT WORKS
The ingredients in this feminine hygiene product also neutralize skunk odor.

STINKING TO HIGH HEAVEN
- Before spraying an enemy, the striped skunk stamps its front feet and hisses or growls.
- A skunk can spray its foul-smelling musk accurately to a distance of up to 12 feet. The pungent odor lingers for several days.
- Skunks are nocturnal—active during the night, asleep during the day.
- To prevent skunks from building a den in your yard or moving in under your house or deck, clear away brush and wood piles, cut back overgrown shrubbery, seal off any potential entrances to under your house or deck, don't leave pet food outside overnight, and keep outdoor garbage cans sealed securely.
- Skunks are nocturnal, so if skunks have taken up residence under your house, wait until dark (when the skunks leave to prowl the neighborhood) to seal up any entrance holes. If you suspect the adult skunks

have left their young behind, call in a pest control specialist or wait until fall or winter for the babies to grow older and go out at night.

- To make sure skunks have left their den beneath your home (before blocking off the entrance), sprinkle a light, even coat of flour or cornstarch in front of the entry. Soon after dark, examine the flour or cornstarch for paw prints indicating that the skunks have gone out for the evening.

- To chase a skunk out from under your house, or from inside a garage or storage shed, simply sprinkle perfume or aftershave lotion around the area. You can also cut off the foot from a clean, used pair of panty hose, saturate some cotton balls with the perfume or aftershave lotion, place them inside the sachet, tie and knot, and hang it anywhere you wish to fend off skunks. Or unscrew a deodorant stick from its dispenser, use a knife to slice the deodorant stick into chunks, and toss them in whatever space you wish the skunks to abandon. Fragrance repels skunks.

- Skunks carry a variety of diseases, including rabies, canine distemper, and canine hepatitis.

- No matter how many times a dog gets sprayed by skunks, it will confront a skunk whenever the opportunity arises.

COME OUT SMELLING LIKE A ROSE

- While working as a chemist at Molex, Inc., Paul Krebaum of Lisle, Illinois, concocted a solution to subdue the horrible reek of hydrogen sulfide gas. He modified the formula so a colleague could use the solution as a skunk remedy. *Chemical & Engineering News* reported the recipe in 1993. In a bucket, mix ¼ cup of baking soda, 1 quart of hydrogen peroxide, and 1 teaspoon of dishwashing liquid. Use a scrub brush to work this solution into your skin and hair (or your skunked pet's fur, and then rinse well). This same solution also neutralizes skunk odor from furniture, carpets, and walls. Apply the solution to items contaminated by skunk odor, wait for the smell to dissipate, and rinse clean.

- Another way to combat skunk odor: Empty two 1-quart cans of tomato juice into a bucket and sponge the juice full-strength all over your body and face and through your hair while sitting in a bathtub with the drain plugged. Then fill the bathtub with water and soak in the diluted tomato juice for 15 minutes, and rinse clean. To deodorize a pet, pour tomato soup over the animal and rub it in. Sponge it over the pet's face. Rinse and repeat.

How to Seal Your Home from Chemical Weapons with Duct Tape

WHAT YOU NEED

- Bandana, handkerchief, cloth, or coffee filter
- Plastic sheeting (or plastic trash bags)
- Duct tape
- Scissors
- Aluminum foil or waxed paper

WHAT TO DO

1. The moment you learn that a lethal chemical plume has been released in your vicinity, evacuate the contaminated area, if possible, or move indoors to limit exposure.
2. Close and lock exterior doors and windows to prevent anyone from entering or leaving after you seal the house.
3. Cover your mouth and nose with a bandana, handkerchief, cloth, or even coffee filter.
4. Close all vents to the outside and shut the fireplace damper.
5. Turn off all air conditioners, heaters, fans, and ventilation systems to prevent circulation of air.
6. Seal all windows and doors with plastic sheeting and duct tape. (If you don't have or run short of plastic sheeting, slice open the bottom and one side of plastic trash bags to create large plastic sheets.)
7. Use aluminum foil or waxed paper to seal around air conditioner vents, kitchen and bathroom exhaust fans, and clothes dryer vents.
8. Most chemical toxins delivered in gas form are heavier than air and tend to stay close to the ground, meaning you should move all your necessary supplies to an interior room in the top floor of your house with access to a bathroom. Or choose an upstairs room with the least number of windows and doors. Avoid selecting a room with a window or wall air conditioner.
9. Once you're locked in the room, place rolled-up towels at the bottom of doors to limit the air circulation within the house, and seal off conduits into the room (including the key hole) with duct tape and plastic sheeting.

HOW IT WORKS
The duct tape, plastic, aluminum foil, and waxed paper create an airlock in your house, preventing chemicals from entering the living space.

A BREATH OF FRESH AIR
- Allow 10 square feet of floor space per person in order to provide sufficient air to prevent carbon dioxide buildup for up to 5 hours. Sunlight and winds would dilute many chemical agents within a few hours, so you would be confined to the inner room only until the chemical cloud dissipates.
- Place exposed clothing and shoes in tightly sealed containers.
- To decontaminate your skin, mix 1 part bleach to 10 parts water and scrub with the solution to reduce the possibility of absorbing a chemical agent through the skin. If water is unavailable, stand in a bathtub or shower stall and liberally sprinkle flour over the affected skin. Wait 30 seconds for the flour to absorb the chemical agent and then, wearing rubber gloves, use a rag to brush off the flour.
- Chemical toxins tend to produce immediate symptoms. Biological agents usually take several days before producing symptoms. If you have been exposed to either, seek immediate medical attention.

8

QUICK GETAWAYS

Vicious thugs are chasing after you. You jump in your car and turn the key, only to discover you've got a dead battery, a leaking gas tank, and a broken fan belt. Can aspirin, chewing gum, and panty hose save the day? Yes, if you work quickly! (Of course, you might want to consider taking the bus instead.)

How to Start a Dead Car Battery with Aspirin

WHAT YOU NEED

- Rubber gloves
- Screwdriver
- Aspirin tablets
- Water

WHAT TO DO

1. To revive a dead car battery, wear rubber gloves and carefully pry the cell cover off the battery with a screwdriver (provided the lid is not sealed permanently shut). *Be careful not to get battery acid on yourself.*
2. Crush two aspirin tablets for each cell of the battery.
3. Put the powder in the battery.
4. Add water to fill the battery to the proper level.
5. Reseal the cell cover.
6. Let sit for no more than 1 hour and start the engine.
7. Drive directly to a service station to replace the battery.

HOW IT WORKS

The acetylsalicylic acid in the aspirin combines with the sulfuric acid in the battery to allow one more charge—enough to get you to a service station. The water helps restore the electrolyte in the battery.

RECHARGING YOUR BATTERIES

- Wondering where you might find aspirin if your car battery conks out in the middle of nowhere? Check your first aid kit.
- The aspirin gives your battery a boost but will shorten the overall lifespan of the battery.
- The typical car battery contains six cells, each generating roughly 2 volts for a total of 12 volts. To start the engine, a battery must discharge approximately 12 volts at 200 amps.

How to Revive a Dead Car Battery with Epsom Salt

WHAT YOU NEED

- 4 tablespoons of Epsom salt
- ½ cup of distilled water
- Safety goggles
- Rubber gloves
- Screwdriver
- Measuring spoons

WHAT TO DO

1. Provided the battery lid is not sealed permanently shut, dissolve 4 tablespoons of Epsom salt in just enough distilled water (not tap water) to create a liquid.
2. Wearing safety goggles and rubber gloves, use a screwdriver to carefully remove a cap from the cells of the battery.
3. Pour 1 tablespoon of the solution into each of the six cells of the battery.
4. Replace the cap firmly.
5. Recharge the battery on slow charge for 24 hours.

HOW IT WORKS

Adding Epsom salt to the electrolyte of a lead acid battery can reduce the buildup of lead sulfate on the plates and improve the overall battery performance.

WITH A PINCH OF SALT

- Car batteries contain sulfuric acid, a highly caustic acid compound. If you get battery acid on your skin, flush with water immediately.
- Epsom salt is nothing more than pure magnesium sulfate in powder form.
- Where did Epsom salt get its catchy name? From the springs in Epsom, England, where it was first mined.

How to Plug a Gas Tank Leak with Chewing Gum

WHAT YOU NEED

- Piece of chewing gum
- Duct tape (optional)

WHAT TO DO

1. To repair a leaking gas tank temporarily, chew a piece of chewing gum or bubble gum until all the sugar is gone and then use it to patch the hole by pushing it into and around the rupture.
2. To fortify the patch, cover the gum with a strip of duct tape.
3. After every hour of driving, add an additional piece of chewing gum to the patch.

HOW IT WORKS

The gasoline acts as a catalyst, hardening the gum into an epoxy-like solid that patches the hole long enough for you to drive to a repair shop.

GUM UP THE WORKS

- In 1918, Mrs. Ernest Byfield and Miss Elaine Rosenthal, two new motor mechanics in the motor supply corps, got stuck on a country road in Illinois due to a gas tank leak. They purchased chewing gum at a nearby store and chewed all 110 sticks to patch the gas tank and get the car back on the road again.
- In his book, *Autobiography of a Soldier: Microphone in Hand*, Master Sergeant Garry L. Lyon recalls patching a leaking gas tank on his 1962 Ford station wagon with chewing gum in 30-degrees-below-zero weather in Dawson Creek, Canada. "I smashed the wad of gum onto the leak," he wrote, "pressing it out as best I could. Seconds later, it froze and the leak stopped. Now you're probably thinking the same thing I was ... as soon as I got into warm weather, that leak would pop right back up. Well, I continued my trip, stopped at Fort Lewis for a couple of days, drove home to Los Angeles, messed around for a week or so, and traded that old wagon on a 1956 Studebaker, Silver Hawk. The chewing gum was still in place and there wasn't a sign of gas leak."

How to Repair a Broken Fan Belt with Panty Hose

WHAT YOU NEED

- Scissors or knife
- Clean, used pair of panty hose

WHAT TO DO

1. If the fan belt breaks on your car while on you're on the road and unable to get help, cut off one leg from a clean, used pair of panty hose.
2. Feed the leg of the panty hose around the appropriate spindles, pull the ends together, making the nylon loop taut, and tie the two ends into a tight double knot.
3. Using a pair of scissors or a knife, cut off the excess hose after the knot.

HOW IT WORKS

The panty hose leg doubles as a fan belt, re-engaging the alternator and water-pump drives, enabling you to drive the car to a gas station or automotive store to get a proper replacement.

TIGHTENING YOUR BELT

- If the panty hose leg needs more traction to work as a fan belt, tie a series of knots along the length of the leg.
- You can also use a pair of panty hose as a replacement for a windshield wiper blade. Simply wrap the panty hose around the metal wiper arm several times and knot in place.
- During the East African Safari—an annual rally through Tanzania, Uganda, and Kenya—Irish racecar driver Rosemary Smith broke a fan belt in a remote section of the race. "She took off her panty hose and made a fan belt of it, and raced the rest of the day with it in place," according to Seán ÓLaoire, author of *A Sensible God*.
- Discussing fan belts, the 2009 travel guidebook *Let's Go: Roadtripping USA on a Budget* by Harvard Student Agencies states: "In an emergency, panty hose can serve as a temporary yet sultry substitute."

How to Fix a Leaky Car Radiator with Black Pepper

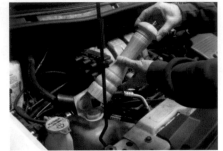

WHAT YOU NEED

- Teaspoon
- Black pepper

WHAT TO DO

1. To stop a small leak in a radiator, first **let the engine cool** (to avoid being scalded by hot water or steam), and carefully remove the radiator cap.
2. Add a teaspoon of ground black pepper to the coolant in your radiator.
3. Replace the radiator cap (to allow pressure to build up in the radiator).

HOW IT WORKS

The pepper sinks to the bottom, finds its way into small pinholes, and expands, filling them and temporarily plugging the hole—until you can get to a repair shop.

EGGSTENUATING CIRCUMSTANCES

- If you don't have any pepper, add 2 tablespoons of dry mustard powder (such as Coleman's Mustard) to the coolant in the radiator. Like the pepper, the mustard powder will expand, migrate to the pinholes, and seal them temporarily, giving you enough time to get the car to a repair shop. The excess dissolves in the coolant.
- In a dire emergency, crack open one or two raw eggs, separate the yolk, and pour the egg white into the radiator (without any egg shells), and recap the radiator. The hot water in the radiator will cook the egg white, and the pressure will force the solidified egg white into the pinholes in the radiator, temporarily plugging the leak until you can get to a repair shop. (Avoid pouring the yolk into the radiator, which could plug up the heater core.)
- To avoid burning your hands on the radiator cap if you don't have a glove or oven mitt, slip one or two socks over your hand to create an instant glove. Or fold a bandana several times to create a makeshift potholder.

How to Clean Corrosion from Car Battery Terminals with Coca-Cola

WHAT YOU NEED
- Rubber gloves
- Can of Coca-Cola
- Clean, used toothbrush (or wire brush)
- Water
- Paper towel

WHAT TO DO
1. Wearing rubber gloves, carefully disconnect the battery cables, removing the negative cable first to avoid getting a shock. If corrosion holds the cables in place, slowly pour a small amount of Coca-Cola around the terminals. When the Coke stops fizzing, remove the cables.
2. Secure both cables away from the battery terminals.
3. Slowly pour a small amount of Coca Cola over the white powder on the terminals.
4. Wait for the Coke to stop fizzing.
5. Pour a small amount of Coke over the metal connectors on the battery cables to remove any remaining corrosion.
6. Use the toothbrush to scrub away any remaining corrosion on the terminals or metal connectors.
7. Pour a small amount of water over the terminals and metal connectors to rinse away the Coca-Cola and any debris.
8. Dry the terminals and connectors thoroughly with a paper towel.
9. Reattach the positive cable to the positive battery terminal, followed by the negative cable to the negative battery terminal. (Typically, the negative terminal will spark when you reconnect the cable.)

HOW IT WORKS
The carbonic acid in Coca-Cola fizzes away the calcium corrosion.

A TERMINAL SITUATION
- For another way to clean corrosion from car battery terminals, mix 2 teaspoons of baking soda in 1 cup of water, pour the solution over the battery cable connections, and use a clean, used toothbrush to

scrub the encrusted areas clean. After the baking soda bubbles away the corrosion, wash the terminals clean with water.

- To prevent clean car battery terminals from corroding, coat the terminals with petroleum jelly or lip balm (any flavor will do).
- When you disconnect your car's battery cables to work on the battery, you can prevent the end of the battery cable connector from touching the battery terminal by cutting a slit in two tennis balls and carefully inserting each battery connector into its own rubber ball.

How to Create Traction for a Car Stuck in Snow with Carpet Mats

WHAT YOU NEED

- 2 carpet mats (from inside the car)

WHAT TO DO

1. Before you start the engine, *clear any snow away from the tailpipe*. Otherwise, a blocked tailpipe will send deadly carbon monoxide gas inside the car.
2. Dig away as much excess snow and ice from in front of the tires as possible.
3. Turn the steering wheel to straighten the front wheels (provided no objects obstruct the path of the car).
4. Wedge the floor mats in front of the rear tires of a rear-wheel-drive vehicle, the front tires of front-wheel-drive vehicle, and either set of tires of a four-wheel-drive vehicle).
5. Making sure all spectators stand clear of the tires (in case the carpet mats spin out from under the tires), gently press the gas pedal.

HOW IT WORKS

The carpet mats provide traction. Be aware, however, that the tires will most likely destroy the mats.

SETTING THE WHEELS IN MOTION

- You can also free a car from the snow by placing tree branches under the tires.
- To create traction for tires stuck in snow or ice, pour a little bleach directly on the tire, wait 1 minute, and then try to move the car. The bleach chemically reacts with the rubber tire, making it stickier and increasing the traction.
- Pour unused kitty litter in front of your tires stuck in the snow or ice. The cat litter creates traction under the wheels, enabling it to get out of the situation.
- If you don't have an ice scraper, you can use an expired credit card, a plastic paint scraper, or a plastic or Teflon-coated kitchen spatula.

How to Repair a Flat Tire with Superglue

WHAT YOU NEED
- Superglue

WHAT TO DO
1. To temporarily patch a small hole in a flat tire (caused by an errant nail or screw), locate the puncture on the tire.
2. Insert the nozzle of the superglue tube into the puncture and squeeze a few drops of superglue through the inside of the puncture and into the tire.
3. Remove the nozzle of the superglue tube from the puncture and cover the puncture hole with the glue.
4. Let it sit for 5 minutes.
5. Inflate the tire with air and drive to the nearest repair shop to have the tire properly repaired or replaced.

HOW IT WORKS
The cyanoacrylate is a strong, fast-acting adhesive capable of sealing a puncture in a rubber tire—temporarily. Unfortunately, cyanoacrylate dries solid, making it inflexible and brittle. When the rubber tire flexes and the temperature of the tire tread cause the rubber to expand and contract, the bond between the rubber and the superglue could break or crack.

STICKY FINGERS
- Superglue cannot be used to fill holes because thin layers of cyanoacrylate bond far more effectively than thick layers. If the puncture has created a gap, fill the gap with baking soda and then add a few drops of superglue over the baking soda. The cyanoacrylate glue and baking soda harden into a lightweight adhesive filler. **Caution:** the reaction between cyanoacrylate and baking soda produces heat and noxious vapors.
- Early models of the Volkswagen Beetle used the air pressure from the spare tire to shoot water from the windshield washer reservoir.
- To locate a puncture in a tire, use an air compressor to fill the tire with air. Pour 1 teaspoon of dish detergent into an empty spray bottle, fill the rest of the bottle with water, and shake well. Spray the solution over the tires. The pressurized air escaping from the tire will create bubbles in the liquid at the site of the puncture.

Acknowledgments

I am grateful to my editor at Chicago Review Press, Jerome Pohlen, for championing my cause and making this book a labor of love. I am also deeply thankful to ace project editor Devon Freeny, designer Andrew Brozyna, my agent Laurie Abkemeier, researcher and photographer Debbie Green, photographer Carrie Bruder, Wayne Shapiro, and my manager Barb North. Above all, all my love to Debbie, Ashley, and Julia.

Bibliography

Books and Articles

"An Alarm You Can Make" by G. Taylor Urquhart. *Boy's Life*, April 1976, 68.

"Armed Robber Steals Potato Chips" by *Tracy (CA) Press*. January 12, 2009.

Autobiography of a Soldier: Microphone in Hand by Garry L. Lyon. Pittsburgh: Rosedog Books, 2009.

"Bringing NASA Down to Earth" by Tom Huntington. *American Heritage*, Fall 2008.

"Chewing Gum Used by Women to Stop Leak in Gas Tank" by *Deseret News*. December 27, 1918.

The CIA Lockpicking Manual by the Central Intelligence Agency. New York: Skyhorse, 2011.

"The Claim: Listerine Can Ward Off a Swarm of Mosquitoes" by Anahad O'Connor. *New York Times*, June 24, 2008.

The Complete Terrorism Survival Guide: How to Travel, Work and Live in Safety by Juval Aviv. Huntington, NY: Juris, 2003.

"A Dying Race" by *Rodney and Otamatea (NZ) Times*. May 8, 1912.

Emergency Food, Storage & Survival Handbook: Everything You Need to Know to Keep Your Family Safe in a Crisis by Peggy Layton. New York: Three Rivers, 2002.

The Encyclopedia of Two-Hour Craft Projects by Leslie Allen, Patrice Boerens, Linda Durbano, et al. New York: Main Street, 1997.

Explosive Loading of Engineering Structures by P. S. Bulson. Boca Raton, FL: CRC, 1997.

"Extra-Alarm Fire at Grocery Store in Stone Park" by Matt Walberg, Chuck Berman, and Rosemary Regina Sobol. *Chicago Tribune*, May 28, 2013.

"For Troops, Panty Hose Are a Defensive Weapon" by Tim Blangger. *Chicago Tribune*, April 6, 2003.

The Formula Book by Norman Stark. New York: Avon, 1975.

"German Puts Out Cigarette with Fire Extinguisher" by Dave Graham. Reuters, February 19, 2008.

"Hold Viet War Vet in Kidnap" by United Press International. *Times-Union*, July 21, 1972.

"How to Stitch Your Own Gash" by Bryan Doonan. *Surfing Magazine* 41, no. 7.

How to Survive Anything, Anywhere: A Handbook of Survival Skills for Every Scenario and Environment by Chris McNab. Camden, ME: McGraw Hill, 2004.

How to Survive Anywhere: A Guide for Urban, Suburban, Rural, and Wilderness Environments by Christopher Nyerges. Mechanicsburg, PA: Stackpole Books, 2006.

"How Uplifting: The Bra That Can Be Converted into a Life-Saving Face Mask" by Jody Thompson. *Daily Mail*, September 29, 2010.

"Jogger Suffers Serious Injuries After Running into Tripwire Booby Trap" edited by Sunita Patel-Carstairs. *Telegraph*, September 20, 2013.

"The Man Buried in a Pringles Can" by Jeremy Caplan. *Time*, June 4, 2008.

Manifold Destiny: The One! The Only! Guide to Cooking on Your Car Engine! by Chris Maynard and Bill Scheller. New York: Simon & Schuster, 2008.

"Marijuana Grower Killed—and Nearly Decapitated—by Booby Trap He Set to Protect Plants" by Lee Moran. *New York Daily News*, September 3, 2013.

"Marijuana Stash Discovered at Rehab Facility" by *Beacon News*. July 5, 2013.

"Montreal Smoke Bomb Attack: Four Detained in Assault on Metro System" by Canadian Press. May 11, 2012.

National Geographic Complete Survival Manual by Michael S. Sweeney. Washington, DC: National Geographic, 2009.

"Not So Silly String in Iraq" by Ellin Martens. *Time*, November 19, 2007.

"One Is Not Amused by Prince Harry's Smokebomb Prank" by Lucy Ballinger. *Daily Mail*, September 24, 2006.

Painting Secrets from Brian Santos, the Wall Wizard by Brian Santos. Des Moines, IA: Meredith Books, 2004.

A Paranoid's Ultimate Survival Guide: Dust Mites to Meteorites, Tsunamis to Ticks, Killer Clouds to Jelly Fish, Solar Flares to Salmonella by Patricia Barnes-Svarney and Thomas Eugene Svarney. Amherst, NY: Prometheus Books, 2002.

"Publication Bias and Time-Trend Bias in Meta-Analysis of Bicycle Helmet Efficacy: A Re-analysis of Attewell, Glase and McFadden, 2001" by Rune Elvik. *Accident Analysis and Prevention* 43 (May 2011): 1245–51.

"Reflecting on Space Benefits: A Shining Example" by NASA. September 2006.

Re/Uses: 2,133 Ways to Recycle and Reuse the Things You Ordinarily Throw Away by Carolyn Jabs. New York: Crown, 1982.

The Secrets of Houdini by John Clucas Cannell. Mineola, NY: Courier Dover, 1931.

"A Serious Use for Silly String" by Rebecca Santana. Associated Press, December 7, 2006.

"$60K Settles Staten Island Cop's Suit for Slip-and-Fall" by Frank Donnelly. *Staten Island Advance*, July 10, 2012.

Special Forces Survival Guide: Wilderness Survival Skills from the World's Most Elite Military Units by Chris McNab. Berkeley, CA: Ulysses, 2008.

Stay Alive! Survival Skills You Need by John D. McCann. Iola, WI: Krause, 2011.

Survival by Hugh C. McDonald. New York: Ballantine Books, 1982.

Tammy Wynette: Tragic Country Queen by Jimmy McDonough. New York: Viking, 2010.

"Thyroid Cancer a Hazard from Radioactive Iodine Emitted by Japan's Failing Nuclear Power Plants" by Patrick J. Skerrett. *Harvard Health*, March 14, 2011.

"Trio's Mischief Results in Store Blaze" by Bob LaMendola. *Fort Lauderdale Sun Sentinel*, November 10, 1991.

The Ultimate Survival Manual: 333 Skills That Will Get You Out Alive by Rich Johnson and the editors of *Outdoor Life*. San Francisco: Weldon Owen, 2012.

"U.S. Hijackings Since May 1" by United Press International. *Sarasota Herald Tribune*, July 20, 1983.

"U.S. Soldiers' Options Limited to Protect Afghans from Taliban" by Philip Smucker. McClatchy Newspapers, May 25, 2009.

Vinegar, Duct Tape, Milk Jugs & More: 1,001 Ingenious Ways to Use Common Household Items to Repair, Restore, Revive, or Replace Just About Everything in Your Life by Earl Proulx and the editors of *Yankee Magazine*. Emmaus, PA: Rodale, 1999.
"Who Made That Clothespin?" by Hilary Greenbaum and Charles Wilson. *New York Times*, May 11, 2012.

Websites

Car Talk Blog: "I Put Sugar in My Husband's Gas Tank"
www.cartalk.com/content/i-put-sugar-my-husbands-gas-tank
The Decoy Paratrooper Dummy History Site (Archived)
http://web.archive.org/web/20100326052243/http://home.att
.net/~1.elliott/paratrooperdummyhistorysite.html
The Emergency Bra
www.ebbra.com
Emergency Preparedness and Response: Potassium Iodide (KI)
www.bt.cdc.gov/radiation/ki.asp#howGiven
Greg's Wireless Networking Info Page: "How to Build a Tin Can Waveguide WiFi Antenna"
www.turnpoint.net/wireless/cantennahowto.html
Homepage of Frank Dörenberg: "My Home-Built Slinky Dipole Antenna"
www.nonstopsystems.com/radio/frank_radio_antenna.htm
The National Terror Alert Response Center: "Chemical Attack"
www.nationalterroralert.com/chemicalattack/
Scouting in Canada: Homemade Equipment
www.scoutscan.com/scouts/homemade.html

About Joey Green

Joey Green is a walking encyclopedia of quirky yet ingenious household hints. A former contributing editor to *National Lampoon* and a former advertising copywriter at J. Walter Thompson, Joey has written television commercials for Burger King and Walt Disney World, and he won a Clio for a print ad he created for Eastman Kodak before launching his career as a bestselling author.

Joey has appeared on dozens of national television shows, including *The Tonight Show with Jay Leno*, *Good Morning America*, and *The View*. He has been profiled in the *New York Times*, *People*, the *Los Angeles Times*, the *Washington Post*, and *USA Today*, and he has been interviewed on hundreds of radio shows.

A native of Miami, Florida, and a graduate of Cornell University (where he founded the campus humor magazine, the *Cornell Lunatic*, still publishing to this very day), he lives in Los Angeles.

Other Books by Joey Green

- *Happy Accidents*
- *Contrary to Popular Belief*
- *Joey Green's Cleaning Magic*
- *Joey Green's Amazing Pet Cures*
- *Joey Green's Magic Health Remedies*
- *Weird & Wonderful Christmas*
- *The Ultimate Mad Scientist Handbook*
- *Joey Green's Kitchen Magic*
- *Dumb History: The Stupidest Mistakes Ever Made*

- *Selling Out: If Famous Authors Wrote Advertising*
- *Joey Green's Fix-It Magic*
- *Joey Green's Gardening Magic*
- *You Know You've Reached Middle Age If . . .*
- *Clean It! Fix It! Eat It!*
- *Marx & Lennon: The Parallel Sayings*
- *Too Old for MySpace, Too Young for Medicare*